BILLY ROCHE

Billy Roche began his career as a singer/musician, forming
The Roach Band in the late seventies. His first novel, *Tumbling
Down,* was published by Wolfhound Press in 1986. His first
play, A *Handful of Stars*, was staged at the Bush Theatre,
London, in 1988, where it won the John Whiting, Plays and
Players and Thames Television Awards. This was followed at
the same theatre by *Poor Beast in the Rain* in 1990 (George
Devine Award) and *Belfry* in 1992 (Charrington Fringe and
Time Out Awards). All three plays became known as *The
Wexford Trilogy* and were performed in their entirety at the
Bush, the Peacock in Dublin and the Theatre Royal, Wexford,
and were subsequently filmed for BBC-TV. His fourth play,
Amphibians, was commissioned by the Royal Shakespeare
Company and performed at the Barbican, London, in 1992.
This was followed by *The Cavalcaders* at the Peacock (1993)
and the Royal Court in London (1994). His screenplay, *Trojan
Eddie*, was directed by Gillies MacKinnon and starred Stephen
Rea and Richard Harris.

As a stage actor Roche has appeared in *A Handful of Stars*
(Bush); *Aristocrats* (Hampstead); *Poor Beast in the Rain*
(Andrews Lane); *The Cavalcaders* (Peacock and Royal Court);
Johnny Nobody (Pocket Theatre); *The Cavalcaders* (Meridian,
Cork) and *Amphibians* (Tin Drum).

His film and TV appearances include *The Bill*, *Everything's
Under Control*, *Strapless*, *Trojan Eddie*, *Most Important*,
Saltwater, *Headwrecker* and *It's All in the Jeans*.

He is currently writer in association with the Abbey Theatre,
Dublin.

Other titles in this series

Lin Coghlan
WAKING

Helen Edmundson
ANNA KARENINA
THE CLEARING
THE MILL ON THE FLOSS
WAR AND PEACE

Barry Hines
KES

Marie Jones
STONES IN HIS POCKETS

Liz Lochhead
MEDEA
PERFECT DAYS

Conor McPherson
DUBLIN CAROL
McPHERSON: FOUR PLAYS
THE WEIR

Gary Mitchell
THE FORCE OF CHANGE
TEARING THE LOOM
    & IN A LITTLE WORLD
    OF OUR OWN
TRUST

Bill Morrison
A LOVE SONG FOR
    ULSTER

Mark O'Rowe
FROM BOTH HIPS
HOWIE THE ROOKIE

Billy Roche
THE WEXFORD TRILOGY

Eugene O'Neill
AH! WILDERNESS
ANNA CHRISTIE &
    THE EMPEROR JONES
DESIRE UNDER THE ELMS
    & THE GREAT GOD
    BROWN
THE HAIRY APE
    & ALL GOD'S CHILLUN
    GOT WINGS
THE ICEMAN COMETH
LONG DAY'S JOURNEY
    INTO NIGHT
A MOON FOR THE
    MISBEGOTTEN
MOURNING BECOMES
    ELECTRA
STRANGE INTERLUDE
A TOUCH OF THE POET

Enda Walsh
DISCO PIGS

David Grant (ed)
THE CRACK IN THE
    EMERALD

Dermot Bolger
THE LAMENT FOR
    ARTHUR CLEARY

Marina Carr
LOW IN THE DARK

Michael Harding
MISOGYNIST

Marie Jones
THE HAMSTER WHEEL

BILLY ROCHE

The Cavalcaders

and

Amphibians

two plays

NICK HERN BOOKS

London

www.nickhernbooks.co.uk

A Nick Hern Book

This double volume of The *Cavalcaders & Amphibians* first published
in Great Britain and the Republic of Ireland in 2001 as a paperback original
by Nick Hern Books, 14 Larden Road, London W3 7ST

The Cavalcaders first published in 1994 by Nick Hern Books,
Amphibians originally published by Warner/Chappell Plays Ltd
in 1992, republished in this revised edition by kind permission
of Josef Weinberger Ltd.

Typeset by Country Setting, Kingsdown, Kent CT14 8ES
Printed by Biddles of Guildford

Front cover photo of the Peacock Theatre production of *The Cavalcaders*
by Charles Collins

Lines from 'Leaning on a Lamppost' by Noel Gay, in *The Cavalcaders*,
reproduced by courtesy of Richard Armitage Ltd, 8/9 Frith Street,
London W1V 5TZ

Music from the songs by Billy Roche in *The Cavalcaders* has been
arranged by Pat Fitzpatrick

A CIP catalogue record for this book is available from the British Library

ISBN 1 85459 463 X

Contents

THE CAVALCADERS

for Tony Doyle

The Cavalcaders was first presented at the Peacock by the Abbey Theatre, Dublin, on 14 July 1993 and subsequently at the Royal Court Theatre, London, on 6 January, 1994. The cast was as follows

TERRY	Tony Doyle
JOSIE	Billy Roche
RORY	Barry Barnes
TED	Gary Lydon
BREDA	Marie Mullen
NUALA	Aisling O'Sullivan

Directed by Robin Lefèvre

Characters

TERRY
JOSIE
RORY
TED
BREDA
NUALA

The play is set in a small town in Ireland. It opens in the present day, flashing back to about seven years ago.

Stage Setting

The main stage setting is an old fashioned shoemaker's shop with a small stocky counter. The shop is cluttered with mended shoes which are stacked on shelves behind the counter and there is a heap of mended and broken uncollected shoes piled up all around from the floor to the ceiling. There are two doors – one leading to the street, the other to a back room and toilet. There is a bench, and tucked away in a corner there is an old battered piano which is usually covered up with a sheet. There is one window, situated behind the counter.

ACT ONE

Lights rise on the shop. TERRY *is standing in the half light which filters in from the street. It is night.* TERRY, *who does not look too well, is dressed in a heavy overcoat and his overall appearance suggests that life has taken its toll on him.*

RORY (*off*). I think this auld fuse is gone, Terry.

TERRY. What's that?

RORY (*entering*). I say I think this auld fuse is gone.

TERRY. There's probably one in that auld drawers there I'd say.

RORY. Yeh reckon? . . . Wait 'til I have a gike . . . Your man thinks he should be in and out of here in about a fortnight yeh know.

TERRY. Who's that?

RORY. Whatshisname – the lad who's doin' the job for me. Oh by the way, while I think of it, if you're wantin' any souvenirs out of this place now, you'd better speak up because it'll all be gone out of here by this time tomorrow. So speak now or forever hold your peace as the fella says. Whist! . . . I'll try this one . . . This place is goin' to be run properly. In and out. None of this hangin' on to stuff for years on end at all. If they're not back to collect the article in question within a month it'll be sold off or given away to charity. (*He goes off.*) . . . Sure there's a shoe in there and it must be there this five years if not more . . . More I'd say!

The light comes on.

How's that?

TERRY. That's her.

RORY. Is that it, yeah?

TERRY. Yeah . . . It's very weak, mind yeh. I'd say that auld
   bulb is goin'.

RORY (*entering*). Huh?

TERRY. I say that auld bulb is nearly bet.

RORY. Yeah? (*He picks up a dusty shoe.*) There it is there
   Terry, look. That must be there this five or six years. That
   used to belong to that one legged man from The Faythe, yeh
   know. Whatshisname – he was an insurance man. Kelly! He
   was in the bed alongside Josie in the hospital that time. The
   poor divil lost his other leg after – the week before he died.
   'There he is now,' says Josie, 'without a leg to stand on.'
   (*He chuckles sadly.*) Poor auld Josie hah! . . . Wait 'til yeh
   see what I'm goin' to do with this place though Terry. A
   new counter along here. And bare floorboards all the way
   out to the door – yeh know all varnished and all. And
   there'll be a bench here for people to sit on while they're
   waitin'.

TERRY. Waitin' for what?

RORY. Their shoes! In and out mate. There's none of this, 'call
   back in three weeks' time,' now yeh know. Those days are
   gone, boy!

TERRY. A Chinese takeaway be Jaysus!

RORY. The shelves'll be all along here. And against the back
   wall there'll be all the machinery and all. Yeh should see the
   gadgets we're gettin' though Terry, I'm not coddin' yeh boy
   . . . Yeh know I can teach a man now in about three weeks
   what it used to take a year to perfect in the auld days. That's
   a fact boy!

TERRY. Yeah but it can't be the same job though can it?

RORY. It is. Better!

TERRY. It couldn't be! I mean where's the skill? Where's the
   attention to detail?

RORY. Attention to detail! Are yeh coddin' me or what? I mean
   do you seriously think now that meself and Ted and Josie

paid any attention to detail? Hah? (*He shakes his head and chuckles.*)

TERRY. I suppose! . . . How's the little one?

RORY. Alright. She's makin' her Communion next month.

TERRY. Is she? Jaysus hah!

RORY. Oh she's a real little madam now the same one! . . . I was lyin' in the bed the other mornin' there though Terry yeh know and next I hears her stirrin' inside the other room. She gets out and toddles across the landin' to the bathroom – a little sleepy head on her. I hear her do a little widdle then flush the toilet after her and then she goes runnin' back to her little warm bed again and I think to meself, 'How did I get her this far at all eh?' Yeh know! . . . They're deadly little sounds though . . . (*He chuckles and basks in the thought of it all.*) . . . I'll go over and get a bulb for that I think because . . . Tell the truth now Terry, I bet you'll be just as glad to see the back of this auld place won't yeh? Hah?

TERRY. Ah I don't know. I mean to say I had me moments here like yeh know.

RORY. Yeah but they were far and few between though Terry weren't they? Hah? admit it now. I tell yeh, yeh already look like a bit of a stranger to the place as it is.

TERRY. Do I?

RORY. Yeah . . . I won't be a minute. Will you be alright there?

TERRY. Yeah.

RORY *leaves. Pause.* TERRY *gazes around him and suddenly an icy shiver seems to creep over him and he whips his head towards the doorway of the back room. He gasps. Pause. He turns to look up at the squinting bulb.*

TERRY. Mmn . . .

The bulb dies. Darkness. Lights rise on the shop. JOSIE *is standing in the middle of the shop with a toilet roll in his hand, singing at the top of his voice.* RORY *and* TED *are up at the window.*

JOSIE (*singing*).
    Oh sole mio
    My arse is sore
    Oh please don't ask me
    To go no more . . .

TED. Look at her. Out of this world ain't she?

RORY. Yeah. Deadly even legs hasn't she? Look, every fella on the street is gawkin' at her. Look at the state of your man Poe the undertaker lookin' at her. He's nearly after jawlockin' himself there.

JOSIE (*singing*). Have mercy

    Oh can't you see . . .

TED. I'd give a week's wages boy just to wake up beside her one mornin', do yeh know that.

RORY. That' s nice of yeh.

TED. No I would though – a week's wages I'd give boy!

JOSIE (*sings*).
    That we surrender
    My arse and me.

    JOSIE *exits to the back room.*

RORY. She is somethin' else though ain't she? Hah? Beautiful Bundoran hah!

    TERRY *enters, younger and more robust than before.*

TERRY. Lord Jaysus ain't that awful – every time I turn me back. The pair of you must think it's a whorehouse I'm runnin' here or somethin', do yeh. Hah? Come down out of there and get back to work out of that.

RORY (*climbing down*). She's deadly boy, I don't care what anyone says.

TERRY. Yes, a whorehouse you must think you're in or somethin'. Who is it, my little bank girl?

RORY. Yeah. Deadly she is boy! I don't care.

TERRY (*climbing up beside* TED). Give us a look at her. She's late today – she must have had a bit of trouble with her balance sheet . . . Oh be the Lort! I'm in love.

TED. What do yeh think of her?

TERRY. What do I think of her? I think she's just . . . What's the word I'm searchin' for?

RORY. Beautiful.

TERRY. Class . . . Do yeh know what I feel now when I look at her?

TED. Yeah – horny.

TERRY. I feel a warm glow inside of me.

RORY. And I second that emotion. I'd marry her in the mornin' boy if she'd have me.

TERRY. Now there's a man who appreciates the finer things in life. Not like you. You're only wantin' to jump on the girl's bones.

TED. That's true. He's right there.

RORY (*sings*). Beautiful Bundoran . . .

TERRY. Did yeh notice that lads, the farther away she gets, the nicer she looks. (To RORY.) I'm goin' to tell your wife on you boy!

RORY. Did yeh see the state of your man Poe lookin' at her?

TERRY. Yeah, he's after catchin' his big chin in the spokes of his bike, look. Funerals'll never be the same again.

RORY. He's probably measurin' her from afar.

BREDA *enters.*

TERRY. Look at the dirt of that window lads.

TED. Yeah, the state of it! (*They both polish and rub.*)

BREDA. I'm not surprised with the pair of you foggin' it up.

RORY (*sings*). Beautiful Bundoran.

TERRY (*climbing down*). Are yeh alright hon?

BREDA. Yeh needn't bother tryin' to plomás me at all boy.

TERRY. Why, what's wrong with yeh?

BREDA. Where's me shoe?

TERRY. What?

BREDA. Me shoe, me shoe. Where is it?

TERRY. Did they not bring that over to you?

BREDA. Well if they did I wouldn't be here lookin' for it now would I? I wouldn't mind but I was goin' to a dinner dance last night and everything. There I was heckin' around me bedroom like a schoolgirl – one shoe on me. I had to get a loan of a pair in the end.

TERRY. I don't know . . . (*He finds the shoe.*)

Did I not tell you to bring that over to Breda when it was mended?

RORY. No, yeh did not.

TED. Yeh needn't bother lookin' at me either.

TERRY. Well I told one of yez. It must have been the other fella I told. It was, too. Hang on Breda.

TERRY goes *off into the back room and we hear him shouting at* JOSIE.

Did I not tell you to bring that shoe over to Breda when it was mended. I wouldn't mind but the woman was waitin' on it too to go to a reunion. She said she was heckin' around the place like a schoolgirl with one shoe on her, lookin' for this. I'm not coddin' yeh if I don't do everythin' meself around here it just don't get done. Well there's goin' to be big changes around here from now on I can tell yeh. Yes, big changes there's goin' to be!

TERRY *returns with the shoe.*

Here y'are Breda – on the house hon.

BREDA. I should think so too. Yeh needn't bother wrappin' it. I'm goin' to wear it. I've a shoe and a slipper on me at the moment. I'm like an orphan of the storm here, so I am.

She sits on the bench to put her shoe on. TERRY *comes out to her.*

TERRY. Yeh could do with a bit of a stitch in that other shoe too Breda I don't mind tellin' yeh.

BREDA. It's alright, I'll get out of here while I'm ahead.

TERRY. No, we'll put a stitch in that for yeh while you're here. Can't have you goin' around the place slipshod now can we? Hah? (*He bends to slip off her shoe.*) Here y'are Ted, put a stitch in that for Breda there will yeh. Do yeh see that stack of shoes there Breda? Take a pair of them for yourself if yeh want – do yeh for knockin' around in.

BREDA. Yeah and end up with someone else's bunions, no thanks.

TERRY (*caressing her feet*). I know a good cure for bunions.

BREDA. I bet yeh do and all.

TERRY. I do though . . . Did anyone ever tell yeh that yeh had lovely little dainty feet?

BREDA. Yeah, someone did mention that to me one time alright.

TERRY. Well he knew what he was talkin' about whoever he was.

RORY. He's real plomásey Breda ain't he? Hah?

BREDA. Shut up you and leave him alone. Go ahead, what were yeh sayin'?

TERRY. What?

RORY. Breda's enjoyin' it.

TERRY. I love women with dainty feet yeh know. It's the first thing I look for.

BREDA. Is it?

TERRY. Mmn . . .

RORY. I love women wheelin' prams. And I love watchin' women drivin'. I love women on bicycles too. And women wearin' glasses. And I like . . .

TED. Yeah alright, we get the message.

> RORY *laughs.* TERRY *and* BREDA *are looking into each other's eyes,* BREDA *is flirting with him with her toes.*

TERRY. Did yeh meet anyone interestin' last night?

BREDA. No.

RORY. What band was playin' at it Breda?

BREDA. The Salinger Brothers.

TERRY. The only three of their kind in captivity hah!

RORY. Yeah. 'She Taught Me to Yodel.'

TED. It's a pity someone wouldn't teach them to sing.

RORY. Did yeh ever notice lads, a great collective sigh goes up every time they play the National Anthem.

TERRY. Hey, don't mock the afflicted boy! . . . So who did yeh dance with all night then?

BREDA. Anyone who asked me.

TERRY. Hah? Jaysus that's not like you, Breda. You used to be very particular.

BREDA. Yeah. That was before the flood though.

> TERRY *chuckles.*

TED. Here y'are Breda, try that on for size.

TERRY. Give it here. (TERRY *takes the shoe and slips it on her foot.*)

TED. You're like Cinderella there Breda.

BREDA. Yeah – after the ball was over!

TERRY. Now . . . How's that.

BREDA (*stands up and wriggles her toes*). Grand . . . I don't owe yeh anythin' then?

TERRY No – not a cent!

BREDA That's good . . . I must come in here more often.

> BREDA *gives a little wave and heads for the door.*

TERRY I'll see yeh hon.

RORY. Bye Breda.

BREDA *leaves.* JOSIE *enters.*

TED. See yeh Breda.

JOSIE. What was that all about?

RORY. Someone forgot to bring Breda's shoe over to her and she was waitin' on it to go to a reunion last night.

JOSIE. Yeah and the auld gom gets the feckin' blame for it here of course . . . (*He puts on his jacket.*) . . . I'm off. Give us me money will yeh. A fiver. (TERRY *throws him a dirty look.*) . . . Two pairs of black there and that brown one behind yeh.

TERRY. Yeah?

JOSIE. And the sandal for whathisname – Friar Tuck.

TERRY. Oh yeah.

JOSIE. He hates payin' money out boy.

TERRY (*wrapping a pair of shoes up in newspaper*). Well listen here, do yeh know what you'll do for me, drop these in to Mrs Kinsella on your way home will yeh. She owes me a fiver. You can keep that then.

JOSIE. I'm not goin' home yet. I'm wantin' to get a couple of large bottles before I go home so . . . I'll tell yeh what I'll do, you give me a sub of three quid and I'll drop these up to her on me way home after . . .

TERRY. It's alright. Here, give them back to me. Here's your fiver. Go ahead.

JOSIE. What? (*He chuckles.*) Are yeh headin' over for one Ted?

TED. Yeah, just a sec . . . (*He puts his tools away.*) Are yeh goin' for a pint Rory?

RORY. No, I'm goin' straight home.

JOSIE. Oh the apron strings boy! The apron strings! Hurry up Ted, will yeh.

TERRY. You fella don't forget we've a practice tonight.

RORY. What time?

TERRY. Seven sharp.

JOSIE. Well make sure it is sharp then.

RORY. Why, have yeh a heavy date on or somethin' Josie?

JOSIE. Yeah, a rendezvous with a couple of large bottles. Come on Ted will yeh for Jaysus sake, you're like an auld woman there . . .

RORY. What are we doin' tonight anyway Terry? Anything adventurous in mind?

TERRY. No.

JOSIE. Where do you think yeh are eh boy – in the French Foreign Legion or somethin'? . . . Adventurous! Are yeh right?

TED. Yeah . . .

NUALA *enters as* TED *and* JOSIE *are leaving.*

I hope you have dainty feet, have yeh?

NUALA. What?

JOSIE. She has dainty hands anyway, I can tell yeh.

TED. How do you know?

JOSIE. Because I bought two oranges off of her this mornin' and they were like a couple of melons in her hands and goosegobs in mine, when I took them out of the bag.

TED. Show us. (*He takes her hand.*) They are too! You'll be devoured.

NUALA. What?

TED *bends to kiss her hand.* NUALA *is flattered by it all.*

RORY. Hey Nuala, do you ever get any of the bank clerks comin' into the shop?

NUALA. Yeah, sometimes. Why?

RORY. No reason. Just wonderin'.

JOSIE. Look at Jacques LePouvier, where he is. (*To* TED.) Come on. (*They leave.*)

NUALA. Would yeh have five pounds in small change to spare, Terry?

TERRY. Yeah, no problem . . . You go ahead home, Rory, leave that. Yeh have to be back down by seven, don't forget.

RORY. Yeah right . . . (*He gets his coat.*) . . . Is the shop shut over there or what, Nuala?

NUALA. Yeah, I shut up for about an hour or so. Why, are yeh wantin' somethin'?

RORY. No it's alright. I'll get it in Breens on my way up. I'm just wantin' to get the young one a bar of chocolate or somethin' that's all . . . There's some change down in the bottom drawer there I think, Terry.

TERRY. What? Is there? Oh, right . . .

RORY. Well Nuala, have yeh settled in yet, yeah?

NUALA. Settled in?

RORY. Yeah. To town life, I mean?

NUALA. Oh yeah. More or less.

RORY. That's good. You've got used to our wily ways, hah?

NUALA *smiles and nods. She stares at* RORY *in a vacant sort of way.* RORY *feels a little uneasy beneath her strange gaze.*

Did yeh get it Terry?

TERRY. Yeah. Go ahead.

RORY. Right. I'll see yeh tonight then Terry, eh?

TERRY. Right. Try and get here on time, will yeh. Stop the other fella whingin'.

RORY (*leaving*). OK. See yeh, Nuala.

NUALA. Bye.

Silence. TERRY *looks into* NUALA*'s eyes. Pause. Slowly* NUALA *goes across and locks the door. She pulls down the blind on it too.* TERRY *pulls down the blind on the window. They turn to look at each other. Then* NUALA *begins to walk slowly towards him, coming in behind the counter, rushing into his arms. They kiss and slither to the floor. Lights down. Lights rise.* TERRY *is standing in the half light, the heavy overcoat on him. There is a loud rapping on the door. He goes across and opens it.* TED *and* JOSIE *enter.*

JOSIE (*switching on the light*). What are yeh doin' in the dark, eh boy – playin' with yourself or somethin'?

TERRY. What? I'm only after gettin' here meself. I have the kettle on.

TED. Any sign of the other fella yet?

TERRY. No.

TED. He must be doin' the ironin'.

JOSIE. Well it's seven now. I'm goin' at half eight on the dot. An hour and a half, yeh said.

TERRY. Yeah, yeah, yeah. What are yeh wantin'? Tea or coffee?

TED. I'll have a tea.

TERRY. Josie?

JOSIE. None of them.

TERRY *is behind the counter making the tea.*

TED. Jaysus, she really has Rory by the short and curlies though lads, hasn't she? Hah? He can't stir boy.

JOSIE. Leave the girl alone. She's alright.

TED. Do yeh hear Josie, all of a sudden . . . You'd think he was a rock of sense there or somethin'.

JOSIE *sniggers.* TED *goes and whips the sheet from the piano. He tinkles.*

JOSIE. Have we any shillin's worth talkin' about in the kitty Terry?

TERRY. Yeah, we have a few bob behind us alright, why?

JOSIE. Just wonderin' . . . I don't suppose there's any chance of a . . .

TERRY. No – no chance! . . . We have expenses. Travellin' expenses, cleanin', sheet music . . .

JOSIE. Yeah alright I get the picture. Just askin'.

TED. Ask, for you shall receive hah!

JOSIE. Yeah. How wrong can yeh be! . . .

TED. Did yeh get home at all Terry, no?

TERRY. No.

TED. And did yeh get anything to eat?

TERRY. Yeah I slipped across for a sandwich.

TED. Yeah? . . . There's dedication, boy! I think this auld thing is after slippin' again Terry.

TERRY. Is it?

TED. Yeah. Yeh might get us out your uncle Eamon's auld tunin' fork there, will yeh. Here he is now. It's about time too.

RORY (*entering*). What? But sure it's only gone seven.

TED. Oh yeah!

RORY. What?

TERRY. Rory, what are you wantin' – tea or coffee?

RORY. Coffee.

TERRY. Of course you'd have to be awkward.

RORY. What?

TED. Yeah, awkward arse.

RORY. What's awkward about it?

TERRY. Here . . . Jacques LePouvier! Now, first things first. Where's the suits?

RORY. They're up in my house.

TERRY. Well, take them down to the cleaners tomorrow will yeh? Right?

RORY. Yeah.

TERRY. Don't forget now.

JOSIE. That reminds me, there's an auld button missin' off my jacket too. I must eh . . .

TED. Rory's missus'll sew that back on for yeh, Josie.

RORY. You'll be lucky.

TED. Tell her I'll be up to start those presses for her tomorrow evenin'.

RORY. Yeah, where did I hear that before?

TED. No, I will though. Straight up!

TERRY. The suits'll be left in here after they're cleaned. Everybody come down here to change into them because there's no proper dressin' rooms or anythin' up above. And afterwards come back here again and change back into your own clothes. Do not go into the bar wearin' the suit. It gives a wrong impression.

RORY. Yeah Josie – makin' a holy show of us.

JOSIE. Can we get on with it now?

TED. Yeah come on, let's get on it.

RORY. Yeah, some of us have homes to go to yeh know.

JOSIE. We know!

RORY. Who is this Jacques LePouviarse anyway?

JOSIE. LePouvier.

TERRY. What? Here y'are Ted. (*The tuning fork.*)

JOSIE. He was a French chap who used to come home to Breens every summer. We all thought we were a right crowd of hard chaws until he arrived. We had a couple of pairs of boxin' gloves, yeh know, and we used to be sparrin' one another out on the street and all. Meself and Terry and little Dinky Doyle and all. Well, your man came over boy and he knocked seven kinds of shite out of the whole lot of us, Terry, didn't he?

TERRY. Yeah.

TED. That's nearly a half tone down, Terry. No wonder hah!

TERRY. Mmn . . .

JOSIE. He was as fast. And hard! You'd think your head was goin' to come off your shoulders when he'd hit yeh, that's all . . . Do yeh remember the day he knocked out poor auld Poe Terry? Dead as a cock, boy! Your man Poe got all serious, yeh know, and the next thing Jacques hauls off and hits him a box in the jaw, knocks him as dead as a cock. I'm not coddin' yeh he looked like a corpse in the gutter. Dinky crossed his arms over his chest and sent a message up to his Da to come down and bury him. The laughs of Jacques at that! He was a gas man though, Terry, wasn't he? Hah? Bon Jour your whore tonight for sure hah! All the girls used to be after him, boy – Breda and all.

RORY. Yeah?

JOSIE. Oh yeah. He was a good lookin' fella like, yeh know. Do yeh remember Dinky, Terry? (*He imitates Dinky's boxing stance.*)

TERRY. Yeah . . . I tried to get Rogan to take on Jacques one time. Rogan would've knackered him alright I'd say.

JOSIE. I don't know.

TERRY. Ah but sure Rogan was like chain lightnin' himself, Josie. And hard too! He gave the Bullet O'Brien a run for his money one night, yeh know. And the Bullet was a handy boxer.

JOSIE. Yeah?

TERRY. Oh yeah. Up the back of the C.Y. The blood was pumpin' out of the pair of them I believe.

JOSIE *thinks about it and shrugs.*

RORY. But sure I heard your man Rogan was a fair man for the women himself was he?

JOSIE *throws him a dirty look. An awkward silence.*

JOSIE Poor auld Jacques though hah! . . . He broke one of my teeth too, the bastard! . . .

TERRY *is putting the tuning fork back in its proper place behind the counter.* TED *is playing the scale, singing in harmony to it.* RORY *clears his throat and paces. The others begin to warm up also.* RORY *joins in with* TED, *singing the bass line.* JOSIE *sings 'Carrig River'.* TERRY *comes to join the others around the piano. He coughs and clears his throat etc.*

RORY (*chanting*). Dominic have the biscuits come . . . Dominic have the biscuits come.

JOSIE (*sings*).
'Tis well I do remember when together we did roam.
Through the lonely dells of Carrig
Where the woodcock makes his home.
All nature it is smiling upon each rocky side.

TED. Are yez right?

TERRY. Yeah, go ahead.

TED. Rory?

RORY. Yeah.

TED. What?

RORY. No, hang on though . . . (*He goes to fetch his coffee.*) Right.

TERRY *gives* TED *the bend and they launch into a barber shop version of 'I'm Leaning on the Lamppost on the Corner of the Street'.*

SONG.
I'm Leaning On The Lamppost On The Corner Of The Street
Until A Certain Little Lady Comes By.
Oh Me, Oh My, I Hope That Little Lady Comes By.
She's Absolutely Marvellous And Absolutely Wonderful
That Anyone Can Understand Why
I'm Leaning On The Lamppost On The Corner Of The Street
Until A Certain Little Lady Comes By.

This verse is repeated softly as TERRY *speaks over it.*

TERRY. Hello Ladies And Gentlemen. You're listening to The Cavalcaders. For the next hour or so we will be bringing you a selection of barber shop songs along with some beautiful classic love songs from the world of popular music. I do hope you enjoy the show.

SONG.

I'm Leaning On The Lamppost On The Corner Of The Street

Until A Certain Little Lady Comes By . . .

The song ends. BREDA *enters, carrying a carrier bag which contains a plate of sandwiches and a plate of cakes and a clean tea-towel-come-table-cloth.*

BREDA. Jaysus, is that the time already.

TERRY. What?

RORY. Nice one Breda.

JOSIE. Yeah – very droll Breda.

TED. Make mine with a little cucumber on the side, Breda will yeh.

BREDA. You'll be lucky.

TERRY. Are yeh alright Breda?

BREDA (*going behind the counter*). Yeah.

RORY. Do you always finish like that Ted?

TED. Like what?

RORY. That abrupt like?

TED. I always play it like that. Why?

RORY. No it just sounded a bit whatdoyoucallit like, yeh know.

TERRY *smiles fondly at* BREDA *as she goes calmly about her work.*

TED. What? (TED *demonstrates.* RORY *nods dubiously.*)

JOSIE (*making a face at* RORY *and then to* TED).Come on.

TED (*to* TERRY). One Heart?

TERRY. Yeah.

TED *plays the introduction. They sing.*

One heart broken
One star falling from the sky
One word spoken
My baby's telling me goodbye.
One day, some day
My dreams will all come true you'll see and then
One day, some day
My baby's coming home to me again.

The voices go lilting over one another at this point.
NUALA *appears in the doorway to bask in the sound of*
The Cavalcaders. BREDA *has finished her work setting out*
the plates on the table cloth on the counter, washing the
mugs and making a fresh pot of tea etc.

NUALA. Beautiful isn't it?

BREDA. Mmn.

NUALA. I love that song . . . And everyone just walks on by . . .

BREDA. Yeah! Jaysus in the auld days this whole neighbourhood 'd be hoppin' whenever the boys were rehearsin' here.

NUALA. Yeah?

BREDA Oh yeah. The Cavalcaders! Terry's uncle Eamon was
the boss that time. Terry and Josie were only the garsúns of
the group . . . (*She chuckles.*) . . . The pair of them had an
awful job convincin' Eamon to let them do a few new
numbers. They did, 'Rag Doll,' and , 'Monday, Monday.'
They used to do a right job on 'Monday, Monday.' . . . The
whole street used to be out listenin' to them though, yeh
know – women sittin' on window sills, children skippin' up
and down outside the shop. Even the men would sometimes
come out of the pub with their pints to join in. Yeh know? . . .
And when Terry got married that time The Cavalcaders sang
at the weddin' mass. Terry actually left the altar and went
up into the organ loft so the quartet could sing the Offertory
that Eamon had written. 'We'll Bring You Water.' . . .
Beautiful! . . .

Whatshisname was the best man that day – Rogan! He said in his speech after that Terry was probably the only man present who had ever sung at his own weddin'. 'And judgin' by the face of the bride when he left the altar,' says he, 'he was a lucky man not to be singin' at his own funeral too.' (BREDA *laughs.*) . . . That was probably the first time Terry ever left them alone together, yeh know – on the altar that day! Dangerous enough occupation too as it turned out.

NUALA. What was she like?

BREDA. Hah? Oh I don't know . . . She was a little bit like you – a little bit like me . . .

Pause. NUALA *loses herself in thought. The Cavalcaders are still singing in the background.* BREDA *looks up at* NUALA *and suddenly understands. Lights down. Lights rise on the shop.* TERRY *is sitting on the bench, dressed in his heavy overcoat. He is lost in thought. There is a loud rapping on the door.* TERRY *goes across and opens it.* RORY *enters with the bulb.*

TERRY. Did yeh get it?

RORY. Yeah . . . did that bulb go or what?

TERRY. Yeah.

RORY. Switch off that auld light there Terry, will yeh. . . . (*He climbs up onto the counter to change the bulb.*) . . . What are yeh wantin' to do about that auld piano?

TERRY. I don't know. What kind of shape is she in?

RORY. Oh I don't know. It sounds alright to me anyway.

TERRY *goes across to tinkle the piano.*

RORY. It's not too bad is it?

TERRY. What? No . . . Are you not wantin' to hang on to this for the young one?

RORY. Are yeh coddin' me or somethin'. Me mother 'd do her nut if I brought that yoke into the house. The state of it!

TERRY. I suppose I may hang on to it meself so. Although I'll probably be shot too. But sure . . . This came out of our

little kitchen yeh know. Hard to believe, ain't it? The whole
street was out the day they rolled it down the hill here to the
shop – me uncle Eamon and big Tom Nail and all. Meself
and Josie were only little lads at the time – taggin' along
behind and that – me poor Ma peerin' out from behind the
little half door. A half door be Jaysus! Anyone 'd think I
was talkin' about a hundred years ago or somethin'! The
poor crator was so ashamed of herself that she became just
a little face in that auld dark doorway in the end. Practically
disappeared, she did. Yeh know I can hardly even remember
her dyin'. I mean, if it wasn't for me uncle Eamon I'd 've
been lost altogether. Yeh know Communions and
Confirmations and all the rest of it. Sure he worked wonders
with me really when I think of it – considerin' like!

RORY. Aye? . . . That's her now.

He climbs down and goes across to switch on the light.

But sure maybe it'll start yeh composin' again Terry if
nothin' else hah? Remember that night? Stop the noise says
you! . . . Jaysus they were innocent auld days though Terry
weren't they? Hah?

TERRY. Yeah well, they could have been.

RORY. What?

Suddenly TERRY*'s head whips round and he looks towards
the back room doorway, terror in his eyes.*

What's up?

TERRY. What? Nothin' . . . Jaysus it's warm in here ain't it?

RORY. What?

TERRY (*mopping his brow*). I'm sweatin'.

RORY. You're leakin' boy! . . . Are yeh alright Terry?

TERRY *nods.*

RORY *looks into* TERRY*'s eyes, a little concerned. Then he
goes into the back room.*

TERRY. They say her face was bone white when they found
her yeh know . . .

RORY (*off*). Who's that?

TERRY. Hah?

RORY (*peeping out*). Did you say somethin'?

TERRY *grimaces and turns away.* RORY *eyes him suspiciously and exits. Lights down. Lights rise on the shop.* JOSIE *and* TED *are present, dressed in their stage suits – blazers, black pants, white frilly shirts and bow ties.* JOSIE*'s outfit is in disarray, the bow tie open, etc.* TED *is changing into his street clothes.* RORY*'s stage suit is hanging up close by.* JOSIE *opens a bottle of Guinness just as* RORY *enters with a handful of dripping mugs.*

RORY. I wonder what's keepin' the other fella? He was talkin' to your man Poe as I was comin' down the stairs of the hall. I think he was gettin' another bookin' off of him or somethin'. He's a queer dour lookin' man though ain't he? Poe!

JOSIE. That's for sure.

RORY. He's well named anyway.

JOSIE. Yeah. He's a Poe by name and nature.

RORY. Somethin' queer happened to him when he was young or somethin' didn't it?

JOSIE. Yeah. He found his Da dead down in the cellar – lyin' in a pool of blood. Seemly he walked into the side of a coffin. Hit him right there in the temple. A little pool of blood not the size of your nail they say.

RORY. Jaysus hah? . . . Deep in the dungeon?

JOSIE. Yeah – where the sun don't shine!

RORY *thinks about it all.*

RORY. I don't think Terry'll be over the moon about the way things went tonight do you?

JOSIE. I wouldn't think so, no. But sure what can yeh do? I mean to say they're entitled to sing whatever they want.

RORY. All the same though Josie . . . Are yeh wantin' a coffee Ted?

TED. No thanks.

RORY. Three of our numbers they ripped off. Or was it four?

JOSIE. Three from tonight's programme. Four if you include 'Monday Monday', but sure we weren't goin' to do that tonight anyway.

RORY. Jaysus it was really panic stations there for a while though wasn't it? Hah? (*He laughs.*) Terry was goin' mad tryin' to change the programme round.

JOSIE. 'Oh Lord Jaysus,' says he, 'there's another one gone.' No but the thing that amuses me though is that meself and Terry have been on this group for over twenty years now and we still only know about twenty-five songs – if we're lucky!

RORY. Were you up in my house this evenin' Ted?

TED. Yeah.

RORY. Well?

TED. Ah I didn't get a whole lot done. I hadn't a lot of time after. I made a start on it. I'll go up tomorrow evenin' and get stuck into them.

RORY. Good. I'll have somewhere to hang me hat at long last . . . Jaysus it was a fairly bad auld show all round tonight though lads wasn't it? Where does he get them eh? I'd say he makes a fair few bob out of it, yeh know. He went home in the hearse. His wife was like Morticia in the back! (*He sniggers.*) . . . 'Frank McCarthy the well known memory man and clairvoyant,' says he, 'will not be appearin' due to unforeseen circumstances.' And did yeh ever see anything like that ventriloquist. Read my lips hah!

JOSIE. That's what I say, but sure what can yeh do.

TERRY (*entering*). Did yeh ever see anything like that in all your born days did yeh? Hah?

JOSIE. What?

TERRY. Do yeh know what I call that now? Plagiarism of the highest order, that's what I call that boy!

JOSIE. But sure they're entitled to sing those songs if they want to. I mean to say we didn't write them or anything.

TERRY. They're entitled to sing whatever songs they want, yeah, but they don't have to rip us off do they? I mean to say they must have knocked off five or six of our numbers there tonight.

JOSIE. Four if yeh include, 'Monday Monday', but sure we weren't goin' to do that anyway.

TERRY. Three of our barber shop songs they did. The very same arrangements and all. The same hand movements and everything!

JOSIE. Yeah well, yeh don't need to be Marcel Marceau to figure them out, now do yeh?

TERRY. It's a wonder they didn't have the same suits as us and all and they at it.

JOSIE. Are yeh coddin' me or what?

TERRY. What's that supposed to mean?

RORY. Yeah Josie, what's wrong with them?

JOSIE. We're like four fuckin' waiters goin' around.

TERRY. We're supposed to be like four waiters ain't we?

JOSIE. Are we?

TERRY. Yes, we are.

JOSIE. Oh!

RORY. Yeah, so don't mock the afflicted boy! But sure yeh know what they say Terry, imitation is a form of flattery.

TERRY. A form of heart attack too. I said it to your man Poe afterwards, mind yeh. I mean to say puttin' them on earlier on in the show would have been bad enough but puttin' them on directly before us was absolutely cat melodian altogether.

JOSIE. What did he say?

TERRY. He said he didn't know what they were goin' to do. To tell yeh the truth he wasn't that put out about it.

RORY. Downtown Munich hah!

JOSIE. Is that what they were called?

TERRY. Downtown Mimic'd be more like it.

JOSIE. Did your man give yeh another bookin'?

TERRY. Yeah. Two weeks' time. So hang up those suits properly after yez. We don't want to be havin' to get them cleaned again between this and then . . . The only thing is, this other crowd are goin' to be on the same bill.

JOSIE. Well I was just sayin' to the lads here a few minutes ago the thing I don't understand is you and me must be on this group this twenty years or more and we still only know about twenty-five songs.

TERRY. Yeah well we'll have a few new babies on the agenda the next time we go out I don't mind tellin' yeh.

JOSIE. Yeah? Three years' work in a fortnight be Jaysus!

RORY. Anythin' in mind Terry?

TERRY. We're goin' to write a few numbers ourselves.

JOSIE. Yeh what?

TERRY. We done it before didn't we with 'One Heart Broken'?

JOSIE. Yeah but we had your uncle Eamon to write the music that time though, didn't we.

TERRY. I wrote the words . . . But sure there's a chap there and he's trained in composition. (*He means* TED.)

JOSIE. Yeah – 'A Day At The Seaside!' . . . What's wrong with you anyway, you're very quiet?

TED. What? Nothin'.

JOSIE *eyes him suspiciously.*

RORY. That's a good idea though Terry – a couple of original numbers!

TERRY. What?

JOSIE. What are yeh goin' to write about?

TERRY. What do yeh mean, what am I goin' to write about? Take a look out the window any day of the week and you'll find somethin' to write about. A whole universe of stuff out there and he's wonderin' what we're goin' to write about. I don't know!

JOSIE. All I ever hear any of yez talkin' about is Legs Eleven from the bank goin' by.

RORY. Beautiful Bundoran hah! She was at the concert tonight too. Sittin' in the third row she was with her legs crossed – nearly put me off a couple of times I don't mind tellin' yeh.

JOSIE. Was that what it was?

TERRY. Yeh know the more I think about how cool that fella took my complaint there tonight!

JOSIE. Who's that?

TERRY. Whatshisname, Poe!

RORY. By name and nature! He buried me Da there last year, yeh know.

TERRY. Yeah well, he won't be buryin' me then I don't mind tellin' yeh. A big face on him now like a well slapped arse, the same fella.

RORY. He cut all his wife's hair off one time or somethin', didn't he?

TERRY. Yeah. he was goin' off to some convention or somethin' and he was afraid of his life that she'd go out on the rantan while he was away and he cut all her hair off.

JOSIE. Oh by name and nature boy! Are you headin' over for one Ted?

TED. No, I'm goin' to head on up the hill home.

JOSIE. What? There must be a blue moon out there tonight or somethin', is there?

RORY. I'll come over for one with yeh, Josie.

JOSIE. What?

RORY. Are yeh goin' over for one, Terry?

TERRY. No.

RORY. What?

JOSIE (*singing*). Blue Moon Of Kentucky Keep On Shinin'. . .

RORY. Terry is already composin', are yeh? Inspiration hah?

JOSIE. Perspiration 'd be more like it now I'd say.

RORY. Hey Josie, hang up that suit properly after yeh, will yeh.

JOSIE. It's alright.

RORY. It's not alright.

JOSIE (*mockingly*). It's not alright.

TERRY. Give that other thing a bit of thought though, Ted, will yeh? I mean if we're goin' to move on it we'd nearly need to be doin' somethin' soon like, yeh know.

TED. Yeah alright. I have a couple of chord sequences goin' round in me head alright.

RORY. Lennon and McCartney look out.

JOSIE. Yeah. Bill and Ben, the flowerpot men. Come on.

The three of them leave. Pause. TERRY *goes across and switches on and off the light three times. He goes and sits up on the counter and waits. Lights down. Lights rise on the shop.* TERRY, *dressed in his vest and pants, is lying prone along the counter, a couple of cushions at his back. His shirt and jumper and coat etc are strewn about the place along with some of* NUALA's *clothing. He is leafing his way through a child's copy book. We hear* NUALA *speaking off and soon she enters, in her slip and bare footed.*

NUALA. The Pelican is the noblest bird of them all, yeh know. She sacrifices herself for her young. Yeh see when her children are born and begin to grow up they flap about and beat their wings and that and they hit the mother and father in the face all the time until one of them becomes angry and strikes them back and accidentally kills them. After that the mother sort of mourns for a few days and then on the third

day she'll pierce her breast and open her side and she'll lay
across her little babes, pouring out her blood all over the
dead bodies and this brings them back to life again. That's
what my poem is all about, yeh see. The Noble Pelican! . . .
River Reddens. Swan Serene. Wonders As She Wanders
Through The Dead Of Night. Blood Soaked Morning Stains
The Day. As Two Dead Babes Come Out To Play . . . But
sure there's another one in there about the Rowan Tree. The
Rowan Tree is supposed to possess some sort of mystical
powers, yeh know, to ward off evil spirits or somethin'.
When I was young we used to have one growin' up around
the house. Its branches touched my little bedroom window.
Made me feel really safe – like I was sleepin' in the arms of
a big gentle giant or somethin'. Our house used to look out
on an auld spooky graveyard like, yeh know? Are yeh
alright?

TERRY. Yeah.

She takes his hand.

NUALA. You've cut yourself again.

TERRY. What?

NUALA. You've cut yourself. Why don't yeh wear the gloves I
gave yeh.

TERRY. I do sometimes.

NUALA. I wish yeh would. (*She kisses his hand.*) I really wish
yeh would . . . What are yeh thinkin' about?

TERRY. Nothin'.

NUALA. Yeh never talk to me, Terry. Yeh never tell me
anythin'.

TERRY. I tell yeh all yeh need to know.

NUALA. Yeah but yeh don't say the things I need to hear
though, do yeh? I'm crazy about you, yeh know. You're the
love of my life. I mean it. I love yeh Terry . . . Did yeh hear
what I said to yeh?

TERRY *sighs, rises and begins to dress.*

Yeh treat me so cruel sometimes, Terry. Yeh really do.

TERRY. Jesus Nuala, stop will yeh, and don't start.

NUALA. What's that supposed to mean?

TERRY. What's it supposed to mean? In all the time that you've been comin' over here did yeh ever once hear me say that word?

NUALA. What word?

TERRY. You know what word.

NUALA. Love?

TERRY. Yeah. Did yeh ever hear me say it? (*She shakes her head.*) Did yeh ever hear me mention it – or hint it even? Yeh didn't, did yeh? (*She shakes her head.*) Right. I mean to say you can say it all yeh want. It's your prerogative. Maybe it makes yeh feel good or somethin'. I don't know. Or maybe you need to find justification for all this. But I don't, yeh see.

NUALA. I say it because it's true.

TERRY. No. You say it because yeh want to hear the words reverberatin' back to yeh. You think you're up in the Alps or somewhere. Well you're not in the Alps. You're in the lowlands lows girl – the same as meself!

NUALA. If I thought you didn't love me I swear I think I'd . . .

TERRY. What?

NUALA. I don't know. I'd throw meself off the bridge or somethin'.

TERRY. Now do yeh hear that – that's the very kind of thing now that . . . Do yeh know somethin', I ought to give yeh a back hander for that, that's what I should do. I mean look at yeh. Hangdog! You're twenty-two years of age for Jaysus sake! I'm nearly twice your age and I feel younger than you do.

NUALA. I've given yeh so much, Terry. I've given yeh everythin'. I've poured out my soul to yeh and I hardly know anythin' about you.

TERRY. Well what exactly is it yeh need to know?

NUALA. I don't know.

TERRY. What?

NUALA. I need to know what she looks like.

TERRY. What?

NUALA. Your wife?

TERRY. What about her?

NUALA. I've been told that yeh still carry a photo of her with yeh in your wallet everywhere yeh go.

TERRY. Who told yeh that?

NUALA. Is it true?

TERRY. What if it is?

NUALA. I want to know what she looks like.

TERRY. Why?

NUALA. Because I just need to know that's all.

TERRY. Oh yeh just need to know! Jesus . . . God, give me patience!

NUALA. I found out where she lives, yeh know . . . I found out where she lives and I went to her house to see her.

TERRY. When?

NUALA. One day last week.

TERRY. How did yeh get up there?

NUALA. Took a train.

TERRY. Are you mad or what?

NUALA. Don't say that to me Terry . . . It's alright, yeh needn't worry, I didn't go near her or anything. I just hung around outside the house for a few hours that's all.

TERRY. Yeh didn t see her then?

NUALA *shakes her head sulkily.*

Nobody home?

NUALA. Some fella on a walkin' stick . . . But I do need to know what she looks like though Terry, yeh know. I mean I really need to know what I'm up against.

TERRY. Oh yeh need to know what you're up against! That's different. Why didn't yeh say so. I mean if yeh need to know what you're up against! Well I mean . . .

NUALA. What?

TERRY. Hah? . . . Jesus! (*He paces about irritably.*) Right! Alright. Here. (*Angrily he takes out a photo and forces it upon her.*) Here. There. Now. Now yeh know. Are yeh happy now? Hah? Yeah? Happy? . . . Now do you think for one minute that you can compete against that. Do you seriously think for one minute that you can compete . . .

NUALA. That picture's nearly twenty years old. She don't look like that any more.

TERRY. That's not what I asked yeh. Do yeh think you can compete against it, is what I'm askin' yeh.

NUALA. Yeah I do.

TERRY. How?

NUALA. Easy.

TERRY. How easy?

NUALA. What?

TERRY. How easy, I said. Hah?

NUALA, *in a fit of rage, snatches the photograph from his hand and tears it in two, throwing it on the floor.* TERRY *takes her by the hair and slings her to the ground. He bends to pick up the pieces.*

TERRY. Don't you ever touch anythin' belongin' to me again.

NUALA. She don't look like that now.

TERRY. You're fuckin' neurotic, yeh know. A feckin' fruit cake yeh are.

NUALA. Well at least I'm not walkin' around in someone else's shadow all the time, anyway.

TERRY. What's that supposed to mean?

NUALA. He took her away from you and now you're takin' it out on me. But I'm not the one who needs to be forgiven . . .

TERRY. Do yeh know somethin', all those head shrinkers you're goin' to are beginnin' to take effect on yeh, I think.

NUALA. Because I'm not the one who hurt yeh. I didn't do yeh any wrong Terry . . .

TERRY. But if you're goin' to start analysin' anybody then I'd prefer if yeh picked somebody else, if yeh don't mind. preferably somewhere else . . .

NUALA. Maybe yeh need to forgive yourself for callin' him a friend in the first place.

TERRY. You don't know nothin' about it.

NUALA. I know . . . I know . . .

TERRY. What do yeh know? What is it yeh know?

NUALA. I know that he was supposed to be your best friend and he let yeh down – stole your wife away from yeh, moved in with her above the little baker's shop right across the street there.

TERRY. Ain't that awful what I've to listen to, too . . .

NUALA. And it used to break your heart to have to stand here and look at the two of them goin' in and out every day, holdin' hands and talkin' and laughin' and lookin' at one another and all . . .

TERRY. Two weeks in a funny farm and she thinks she's a professor or somethin'.

NUALA. But he didn't give a toss about you – not a toss. Of course you thought the sun, moon and stars shone out of him. Rogan could do no wrong as far as you were concerned. Rogan did this and Rogan did that and Rogan did the other thing and everybody knows he never did nothin' really. While you were walkin' the slippy pole and swimmin' the river or runnin' races he was standin' there like a duke in blue jeans be Jaysus lookin' at himself in a shop window. A real little shite goin' around if yeh ask me. Couldn't even get his own girl!

TERRY. Oh, you'd know, of course.

NUALA. But unfortunately he's not goin' to bring her back to yeh Terry. I'm sorry to have to be the one to inform yeh and all but . . .

TERRY. The day I need a headbanger like you to tell me how to live my life . . .

NUALA. She's not comin' back to yeh Terry.

TERRY. Is the day I'll lie down and . . .

NUALA. She's not comin' back boy. Yeh may forget about her. She's not comin' back.

TERRY. I know she's not comin' back.

NUALA. Well what are yeh waitin' for then? Hah? What are yeh waitin' for?

TERRY. If you think now for one minute that I'm goin' to stand here and listen to you bullshittin' . . .

NUALA. What are yeh waitin' for?

TERRY. What am I waitin' for? I'll tell yeh what I'm waitin' for. Do yeh want to know what I'm waitin' for? I'm waitin' for you to get the f . . .

Red with rage, hands clenched TERRY *looks around for something to vent his spleen on.* NUALA *watches him calmly. When his rage has passed he stands breathless, holding on to the counter.* NUALA *moves towards him with tender eyes.*

NUALA. I'm the other half of you Terry, you're the other half of me!

TERRY *sighs, chuckling through his exasperation.*

TERRY. I don't think you should come over here any more, Nuala.

NUALA. What?

TERRY. I'm no good for yeh . . . I'm only usin' yeh, sure!

NUALA. Usin' me? What do yeh mean – usin' me?

TERRY. What are yeh wantin' me to do, spell it out for yeh or somethin'? . . . Don't look at me like that. It gives me the creeps when yeh look at me like that. I mean to say that's the very thing now that . . . Look I'm old and you're young. You need somebody young – someone who'll talk to yeh and all, tell yeh things. You need help! Yeh should be able to see through fellas like me anyway. I mean to say, Jesus Christ, I'm practically whatdoyoucallit . . .

NUALA. What do yeh mean, 'usin' me?'

TERRY. Usin' yeh, usin' yeh! I'm only usin' yeh!

TERRY *looks into her fawn-like eyes.*

Look Nuala. Look.

She breaks away.

NUALA. I'm a person, Terry. There's a person inside of me.

TERRY. I know you're a person. if I didn't think there was a person inside of yeh, I wouldn't be tellin' yeh not to come over here any more now, would I? Hah? Now would I?

NUALA. If I thought I'd never see you again I think I'd die.

TERRY. Yeh won't die at all.

NUALA. I would. Give us a chance, Terry. I'll do anythin'.

TERRY. There's no point, Nuala. We've already done everything worth talkin' about and it just don't seem to make any difference. I mean I just don't feel anythin' for yeh like, yeh know. It's not your fault. It's mine. I mean I don't really feel anythin' for anybody anymore yeh know. I mean . . . Ah I don't know . . . Look, just take your things will yeh and go. Go on and don't come over here again.

NUALA. What? (TERRY *turns away from her.*) I have things to offer, Terry. I mean I'm worthy of . . . I mean . . . I'm a worthy person . . . I mean Breda says that he was only a little shit too, yeh know – couldn't even get his own girl!

TERRY. Breda! (*He sniggers softly.*)

NUALA. I know you're really a nice fella at heart, Terry. I know yeh are.

TERRY. I'm not. At heart, or on the surface, or any other way, I'm not a nice fella . I'm not!

NUALA. What?

TERRY. Believe me Nuala, I'm not!

NUALA. I could help yeh to forget about her though Terry, yeh know.

TERRY. What?

NUALA. I said I could help yeh to forget about her.

TERRY. Go ahead home Nuala, will yeh. Go on, get out of here. And stay away from here altogether in the future.

NUALA. You don't really mean that Terry.

TERRY. What?

NUALA. You don't mean that.

TERRY. What is wrong with you eh? I mean where's your pride? Don't you have any pride? I'm tryin' to dump yeh here, and here you are standin' there like an ejit takin' it all. I mean where's your pride, girl? Hah? Hah? I mean, Jesus! . . . Hello, is there anybody in there? Hah?

NUALA. Why are yeh doin' this, Terry?

TERRY. Look, just get out of my life, will yeh. Go on, beat it . . .

NUALA. What?

TERRY. What? What? What? Yeh should see yourself there. You're like a fuckin' puppet on a string or somethin'. The big bulgin' eyes on yeh! So? What?

NUALA. What? To tell yeh the truth Terry, I'm half afraid to go. I mean if I go . . .

TERRY. If yeh go, yeh go. So go!

NUALA. What? Where?

TERRY. What do I care. I mean I don't care where yeh go, do I. Just go. Back to your Da's farm or somewhere. Back to the funny farm if yeh like. I mean I don't care. It makes no odds to me one way or another where you go or don't go, because you don't mean doodle shit to me like, yeh know. I mean I swear I don't give you one second thought from one end of the day to the next. Yeh know? Doodle shit! That's all you are to me.

NUALA. What?

TERRY (*mimics her*). What?

NUALA *suddenly grabs her things and flees tearfully, banging the door behind her.* TERRY *stares towards the doorway. He sighs. Pause.*

God forgive me.

Lights down. Lights rise on the shop. Night. TED *is sitting at the piano.* JOSIE *is sitting on a stool in the middle of the shop, shining The Cavalcaders' shoes.*

JOSIE. I wouldn't mind but everything was goin' grand until Terry's uncle Eamon found his wife out in the hotel yard in the arms of another man and he threw off his coat and went baldheaded for the pair of them. Meself and Terry had to go out after him to try and calm him down. And then when we got back inside here was your man Rogan dancin' with the bride, glidin' around the floor and she gazin' up into his eyes and all. I'm not coddin' yeh, yeh could nearly smell the treachery in the air, boy! I go into the bar then and I overhear the Bullet O' Brien passin' some remark about Terry's ma and I reared up cat melodian on him . . . Jaysus, it was some weddin', boy!

TED. Why, what did he say about her, like?

JOSIE. What? Ah the usual, yeh know. 'Wait 'til I see now,' says he, 'it was either a journey man piano tuner who got her into trouble or some sleazy lookin' banjo player on an auld travellin' dance band. Either way,' says he, 'Terry was destined to be a fairly musical bastard whichever way it went.' . . . I asked the Bullet O'Brien outside and everything over that that day, yeh know. The two of us bet the shit out of one another up at the back of the C.Y. Stop the noise boy! War there was! (*He chuckles.*)

TED. What did yeh make of her?

JOSIE. Who's that? Terry's missus?

TED. Yeah. I mean did yeh think she was a bit of a whore like – goin' off with your man like that in the end?

JOSIE. A whore? No. Ah no, it was nothin' like that or anythin'. I mean she wasn't like Eamon's missus or anythin' like, yeh know . . . She was a queer good lookin' woman though.

TED. Yeah?

JOSIE. Oh yeah. She used to often come in here after they were married. She'd sit up at that auld counter there – the sun streamin' through her hair . . . Jaysus there'd be more botched up jobs after she was gone boy, I'm not coddin' yeh. Poor auld Eamon used to nearly do his nut, that's all. I wouldn't mind, but they say she lives like a nun now. I believe she rarely goes out any more. She tends the garden all the time and nurses him like a nun. You'd hardly think it was the same woman I believe. Or man! What's wrong with yeh?

TED. What? . . . Ah nothin'. I'll tell yeh after.

TERRY *enters from the back room.*

TERRY. I got it Ted. Play us that F Minor again there, will yeh.

TED. What?

TERRY. If Josie sings it straight, right. And you go . . . What is it? . . . It's Sayonara Street. We've Come This Far. Da Da Da Da Da . . . G Sharp Minor . . . Da Da Da Da Da . . . Goodbye . . . Yeh know?

TED. Yeah.

TERRY. Rory stays where he was and I'll go da da da . . . Or whatever. Yeh know? What do yeh think?

RORY *enters with a parcel of fish and chips.*

TED. Yeah . . . Maybe . . .

TERRY. We let it flow then into . . . da da da da . . . Yeh know? And you don't forget to open up your lungs on that change.

TED *nods and begins to jot it down musically.*

JOSIE. What? . . . Yeah . . .

RORY. Stella has a new sign up in the chipper. KNIVES AND FORKS ARE NOT MEDICINE AND SHOULD NOT BE TAKEN AFTER MEALS . . . (*He doles out the fish and chips.*)

JOSIE. Where's me change?

RORY. What? (*He makes a fist at him.*)

TERRY. Good . . . Well Rory, did yeh ask her?

RORY. Yeah.

TERRY. Is she comin' over?

RORY. Yeah, she'll be over in a minute. Listen whatshername is standin' over in the shop doorway too – Nuala! Do yeh want me to ask her over as well or what?

TERRY. What?

RORY. I mean to say, the more the merrier like, yeh know.

TED. Ah no, just leave it at Breda I think.

RORY. What?

TERRY. Yeah, leave it.

RORY. What do you think, Josie?

JOSIE (*eating*). It's immaterial to me.

RORY. Alright.

The men take a break to eat their fish and chips.

TERRY. Are yeh alright, Ted?

TED. Yeah.

JOSIE. Are you still alright for tomorrow?

RORY. Yeah. What time are yeh wantin' to go at?

JOSIE. Oh ten'll do yeh.

RORY. Right. You be down here at ten to ten.

TERRY. What's that?

RORY. I've to drop Josie up to the hospital tomorrow mornin'.

TERRY. What for?

JOSIE. Ah they're goin' to do a few auld tests on me.

TERRY. Well thanks for tellin' me.

JOSIE. Why, what are yeh wantin' to do, come up and hold me hand or somethin'?

TERRY. No, but it'd be nice to know these things, that's all. Go into a pub and somebody asks me how yeh are or somethin', and I haven't a clue what they're talkin' about.

JOSIE. It's only a couple of tests they're doin'. Stop fussin,' will yeh.

TERRY. I'm not fussin' at all. I'd just like to know these things.

JOSIE. Yeah well, now yeh know.

    BREDA *enters.*

    Here she is now . . . The one and only.

TERRY. How are yeh, Breda. Get Breda a stool there Rory, will yeh.

BREDA. What?

RORY. Right.

BREDA. What is this, a private audience or somethin'?

TERRY. Yeah, somethin' like that, Breda.

JOSIE. Well you're more like a guinea pig really Breda, yeh know.

BREDA. Thanks very much, Josie.

RORY. That's nice Breda, ain't it? Hah? Here y'are hon, sit down there and lig do scí . . . Do yeh want me to take off her shoes or anythin', Terry?

BREDA. Me shoes are alright where they are . . .

RORY. Hey, that reminds me, I'm not talkin' to you anyway.

BREDA. Why, what did I do now?

RORY. Runnin' around with French men!

BREDA. What?

JOSIE. I was tellin' him about your man Jacques – the French fella who used to come home to Breens every summer.

BREDA. Oh yeah – Jacques LePouvier, hah! I wonder whatever happened to him.

JOSIE. He's probably in the French Foreign Legion or somewhere, Breda.

RORY. You were mad about him anyway – accordin' to Josie.

BREDA. You must be jokin' me.

JOSIE. All the girls were after him, boy.

BREDA. I'd be made up with him now – a little short arse goin' around.

JOSIE. You wouldn't have said that if yeh had to box him, Breda. Jaysus, he was a lovely boxer boy! Wasn't he, Terry?

TERRY. Yeah. He was good alright.

RORY. Bon jour, yeh whore, tonight for sure hah!

JOSIE. Yeah . . . Are yeh wantin' a few chips, Breda?

BREDA. No thanks.

TERRY. I would've loved to 've seen Rogan taken him on though, yeh know. That would've been a right fight, boy!

JOSIE. Yeah, I wouldn't've minded seein' that one meself, mind yeh.

TERRY. What?

JOSIE. Jacques would've killed him.

TERRY. I don't know Josie! I mean Rogan was hard too, yeh know. And he was queer fast boy!

JOSIE. He had no heart though.

TERRY. Are yeh coddin' me, or what. Rogan was afraid of nothin' or no one, boy!

JOSIE. Jacques would have cut him to ribbons.

TERRY. Yeah well, you didn't know him like I did, Josie.

BREDA *sighs and exits to the back room.*

JOSIE. He was only a bum.

TERRY. What do yeh mean he was only a bum?

JOSIE. He was only a bum. He let everyone down.

TERRY. He didn't let everyone down. He let me down.

JOSIE. Same thing.

TERRY. Anyway who are we to talk, after what we done.

JOSIE. That was different.

TERRY. What was different about it? There was nothin' different about it, Josie!

JOSIE. It was different. We were only young fellas and we only did it the once and then we copped on to yourselves.

TERRY. Yeah, too late for poor old Eamon, though.

JOSIE. Once!

RORY. Jaysus, even Our Lord fell three times lads.

JOSIE *glares at* RORY *and then turns to* TERRY.

JOSIE. What are yeh always harpin' on about that for, anyway? You're always harpin' on about that!

TERRY. I'm not always harpin' on about it at all. I'm just pointin' out to yeh that what he done and what we done was no different, that's all.

JOSIE. I mean, what about her. I mean. She was no saint or anythin'. And your uncle Eamon knew that too, and he should have kept his eye on her. I mean we were only two young fellas. Jesus Christ, I mean! . . . (*He sighs and angrily rolls his food up into a paper ball. He rises and goes behind the counter in search of a waste basket.*) I don't know!

TERRY. What?

JOSIE. Nothin'. Forget it.

TERRY. Huh?

JOSIE. Look, forget it, will yeh.

He wipes the grease from his hands and goes behind the counter. Silence. BREDA *returns with a cup of water. She pops a pill.*

RORY. Are you workin' late tonight Breda, yeah?

BREDA. Yeah . . . What am I'm goin' to hear now, anyway?

RORY. Two new songs, Breda. The first two numbers written for and by The Cavalcaders since 'One Heart Broken'.

BREDA. Yeah? What are they called?

RORY. The first one is called, 'When The Sheets Are Shorter The Bed Looks Longer'. And the second one is entitled, 'No Matter How Far A Fish Swims You'll Never See Him Sweat.'

TED. Yeh can't beat the auld jokes Breda, can yeh?

BREDA. No.

TERRY. Right . . . would yeh like a cup of tea or anythin' Breda, while you're . . .

BREDA. Look, just get on with it, will yeh. I've a woman over there under a dryer and if I don't get her out fairly soon she's goin' to explode on me.

TERRY. Oh right . . . We're all a little bit nervous now. That's why we want to try the new numbers out on you before we go up to the concert tomorrow night like, yeh know.

JOSIE enters.

BREDA. I know all of that. Come on.

TERRY. OK. Are yeh alright, Ted?

TED. Yeah.

TERRY. Alright, fire away, so.

BREDA. Oh, hang on for Nuala.

TERRY. What?

BREDA. Nuala's comin' over. (BREDA *rises and goes to the door to call across the street.*) Nuala! Nuala! Come on . . . She's comin'. She's just shuttin' up the shop.

RORY. Whenever you're ready now, Breda.

BREDA. What? She's comin' . . . But sure, yeh can tell me the history behind the songs while we're waitin', how yeh came to write them and all?

TERRY. What they're about, yeh mean?

BREDA. Yeah.

TERRY. Well the first song I suppose is a sort of a love song. And the second one . . . I suppose it's a sort of a love song too really, ain't it?

TED. Yeah.

BREDA. Two love songs.

RORY. Queer imaginative Breda, ain't we? Hah? (*He chuckles.*)

BREDA. Mmn . . .

RORY. The truth of the matter is Breda, the first song is about Legs Eleven from the bank who goes by here every day, and the second one is about this fella who's tryin' to wriggle his way out of an affair. That's called Sayonara Street. 'Here We Are', says he, 'It's Sayonara Street. We've Come This Far And Now We Are Complete. It's Sayonara Street. Goodbye.' Simple as that! Come in Nuala.

NUALA *enters.*

TERRY. How are yeh, Nuala? Get Nuala a stool there Rory, will yeh. Have we any more stools left?

RORY. What do yeh think we're runnin' here, a picture house or somethin'? Sit up on the counter there, Nuala. Hey Terry, give her a couple of those cushions there. I'm like a butler here. Pierre hah! LePompidou! . . . Lie down there, Nuala.

NUALA. What?

NUALA *props herself up with cushions. She looks lovely.*
TERRY *can't take his eyes off of her. He picks up an extra
cushion and brings it to her.*

TERRY. There y'are, Nuala. Put that at your back hon . . . Did
you change your hair style or somethin', Nuala? It looks
sort of different or somethin'.

NUALA. What? No, I just didn't bother to put it up this
mornin', that's all.

TERRY. It's lovely then. It really suits her like that, Breda,
don't it?

BREDA. Yeah. You've a grand bit of hair, Nuala.

NUALA. Thanks.

Silence.

TED. Are yez right, or what?

TERRY. What? Oh yeah, right Ted. Let her go. You don't
forget what I was sayin' to yeh, now.

JOSIE. Yeah, yeah, come on will yeh.

TERRY. Right Ted.

TED *plays the introduction. They sing.*

SONG. Hey Mister, did yeh see that girl.
  She walks around like she owned the world
  You'd think she owned the world.
  Hey sister, did yeh see that girl
  Her head's so high you'd swear she owned the sky
  You'd think she owned the sky.
  I only wish I knew what day it was
  So I could tell her exactly the way it was
  Or the way that it could be between her and me.
  Hey Mister, did yeh see that girl
  She walks around like she owned the world
  You'd think she owned the world.

Lights down.

ACT TWO

Lights rise on the shoe shop. It is morning. TED *and* RORY
are working behind the counter. TERRY *is busy pottering
around the place, taking stock, etc.*

RORY. No sign of Beautiful Bundoran at the concert at all last
    night Terry, hah?

TERRY. No.

RORY. We'll have to be excommunicatin' that one from the fan
    club I think. She didn't even give in a doctor's note or
    anything, did she?

TERRY. No. Not a word from her, boy!

RORY. After all the time and trouble we put into her, hah?
    That's the thanks we get now!

TERRY. Mmn . . .

RORY. There's that pile of shoes for the orphans, Terry, just in
    case that nun calls in for them while I'm out this mornin'.

TERRY. Right. I hope yeh built up the heels on them, did yeh?

RORY. Yeah.

TERRY. She likes to see high heels before she pays.

RORY. They are high. Sure look at them yourself there. They're
    like stilts . . . Jaysus the boys made a right show of
    themselves last night after though, didn't they? Hah?

TERRY. Who's that?

RORY. Downtown Munich.

TERRY. Oh stop.

RORY. The big fat lad fell off of the stage and everythin', he
    was that drunk. They started arguin' in the dressin' room
    after you were gone Ted, yeh know. The fella with the

glasses kneed the big lad in the bollix and all. I'm not coddin' yeh, he went down like a ton of bricks, boy.

TERRY. But sure, it'll do wonders for his falsetto if nothin' else.

RORY. That's what Josie said too . . . Did you go straight home last night or what, Ted?

TED. Yeah. Ah I couldn't be bothered drinkin' last night. Listen, I'll be back in a minute, Terry. I'm just wantin' to . . .

TERRY. What? Yeah right, Ted.

TED *exits.* RORY *silently wonders about him.* TERRY *shrugs.*

Oh yes, I think we can safely say that we wiped them fellas' eyes for 'em last night alright.

RORY. We saw 'em out of it alright didn't we? The two new numbers didn't go down too bad either, did they?

He exits to the back room.

TERRY. No, not too bad at all, mind yeh. A little more of the same now, I think.

NUALA *enters.* RORY *returns for a tool.*

RORY. How are yeh, Nuala?

NUALA. How are yeh.

TERRY. Nuala.

RORY. I didn t see yeh up at the show last night, Nuala.

NUALA. No, I didn't go.

RORY. Yeh missed it, then.

NUALA. Yeah?

RORY. Yeah. And you were missed too I don't mind tellin' yeh. Wasn't she, Terry?

TERRY. Yeah.

RORY *exits to the back room again.* NUALA *steps up to the counter with a pair of boots to be mended.*

TERRY. How are yeh doin'?

NUALA. Alright.

TERRY. That's good . . . I waited over here for yeh for a while last night, yeh know.

NUALA. Did yeh? . . . I noticed the light on, alright.

TERRY. Why didn't yeh come over?

NUALA. You told me not to.

TERRY. But sure yeh wouldn't want to be mindin' the things I'd say, Nuala. I'd say one thing one minute and the next I'd be . . . Yeh know yourself!

NUALA. All the same.

TERRY. Huh? . . . Look, I'm sorry if I said anything to hurt yeh or anythin'. I get kind of carried away with meself sometimes like, yeh know. I mean yeh know me? Listen Nuala, I really need to see yeh. Really . . . Will yeh come over here later on tonight?

NUALA. I don't know Terry. I don't think so.

TERRY. Why not?

NUALA. You're only usin' me, sure. Yeh said so yourself.

TERRY. Forget what I said, will yeh. Anyway what's all this 'usin' yeh' lark. So I'm usin' you and you're usin' me. I mean to say we're all usin' each another in one way or another.

NUALA. What do yeh mean? I'm not usin' you. I don't use people, Terry.

TERRY. Alright, alright . . . Look, come over to the shop tonight. I'll leave the light on as usual and . . .

NUALA. No. I can't.

TERRY. Why not?

NUALA. I just can't any more, that's all.

TERRY. What do yeh mean, yeh can't any more?

NUALA. I'm seein' someone else, Terry.

TERRY. What? Who?

NUALA. I'd rather not say.

TERRY. Why, is he married or somethin' . . . Do I know him?
(*She nods.*) I know him! . . . By Jaysus, yeh don't let the
grass grow under your feet, do yeh? So where did yeh meet
him, then?

NUALA. He comes into the shop.

TERRY. He comes into the shop! I must know him then . . .
I give up, who is it?

NUALA. I'd rather not say, Terry.

TERRY. Why not?

NUALA. Because he asked me not to.

TERRY. He asked yeh not to! Well how come I never saw yeh
with anybody or anything? I mean where did yeh go with
him like?

NUALA. I don't know. Out of town mostly.

TERRY. Why, does he have a car or somethin'?

NUALA. Sort of.

TERRY. What do yeh mean, sort of? He either has a car or he
hasn't . . . And does he know about me?

NUALA. Yeah.

TERRY. Oh yeh told him about me . . . So he knows about me
but I can't be told about him. And I know this geezer, do I?
(NUALA *nods.*) . . . Well I must look like a right gobshite
to him alright.

NUALA. It's not a competition, Terry.

TERRY. Yeah well, I'll tell yeh what we're goin' to do now.
I'm goin' to wait over here for you tonight, right, and you
needn't bother your arse comin' over at all unless you've
given this fella the shove first. Right? I don't want to see
yeh at all unless you've dumped him. And I want to know

who he is too – and I don't care whether he's married or not. Now if yeh don't come over to see me tonight you can forget about it altogether 'cause we'll be finished as far as I'm concerned. Right? It's up to you. I mean to say I don't want to look like a gobshite at all. No way. Not in this town anyway. Yeh can take it or leave it, Nuala. I mean it makes no odds to me one way or another.

NUALA. Yeah, and then what Terry?

TERRY. What do yeh mean?

NUALA. What are we sneakin' around in the dark all the time for Terry? I'm not married, you're not married. I mean what are we hidin' all the time for?

TERRY. What are yeh talkin' about?

NUALA. Yeh never take me anywhere. We never go anywhere.

TERRY. Oh yeh want to go somewhere. Well where do yeh want to go. I mean where exactly is it yeh want to go?

NUALA. You haven't even told the other lads about me, have yeh. Because you're ashamed of me. You're ashamed to be seen with me.

TERRY. Look Nuala, you don't know this place like I do. I know this place.

NUALA. What's that supposed to mean?

TERRY. You're young and I'm old, that's all.

NUALA. What?

TERRY. What do yeh want from me Nuala? What do yeh want me to say?

NUALA. Nothin'. I just want to be wooed a little bit, Terry, that's all.

TERRY. Alright. So come over here tonight and I'll woo yeh all yeh want.

NUALA. Tch . . . I have to go.

TERRY. You've to go! (TERRY *sighs and scoffs to himself.*)

NUALA. I'm a person Terry. There's someone inside of me too, yeh know. (TERRY *shakes his head and sighs.*) . . . I'll see yeh.

She leaves in a huff just as TED *enters. The two men stand to watch her go.* TED *wonders about it.* RORY *returns.*

TERRY. I don't know!

RORY. What's up, Terry.

TERRY *shakes his head and sighs.*

TERRY. Here, see what's wrong with them there, will yeh. (NUALA*'s boots.*)

RORY. What's wrong with them? What's right with them, yeh mean! I mean, is she serious or what? Look at the state of them. (*He opens up the gaping hole and makes it sing.*) I Wander Down By That Little Babbling Brook. Its Every Ripple Speaks Of Thee . . .

TED. What were yeh sayin' to Nuala there, Terry?

TERRY. What? Nothin'. Why?

TED. Just wonderin'.

RORY. I don't know, lads.

TED *goes back to his bench.* TERRY *watches him suspiciously.*

I was just sayin' there though, Terry, that there was hardly anyone from around here at the concert last night, was there?

TERRY. There was no one from around here at it, sure. Bloody scandalous so it is! Jaysus in the auld days this whole neighbourhood 'd be flockin' in to see The Cavalcaders, so they would.

RORY. Aye?

TERRY. Oh yeah. The Cavalcaders! Stop the noise! But sure when me uncle Eamon wrote the mass that time, the little chapel was burstin' at the seams with people. They were standin' out on the street and everything. And every one of them as proud as punch about it. You'd swear they were after writin' it themselves or somethin'. There was some great characters around here that time though, yeh know. Not like now. There's no real characters around now. A fella turns his hat back to front or somethin' now and they all think he's a great fella . . . Me uncle Eamon was like a god around here that time though, yeh know. They'd nearly get off the path for him, man. Until she got her hands on him, of course. By Jaysus she really sapped the magic out of him alright, boy.

RORY. How do yeh mean?

TERRY. What?

TED *goes out to the back room.* TERRY *watches him. Pause.*

RORY. Jaysus, it'd be great to have that kind of support now though, Terry, wouldn't it? Hah? They stay away in their droves now, don't they? Afraid of their lives that they might enjoy themselves of course, ain't they? Hah?

TERRY. Mmn . . . Does Ted ever ask you for a loan of your car this weather?

RORY. What? Yeah, sometimes yeah. Why?

TERRY. No reason. Just wonderin'.

RORY. What?

JOSIE *enters, a bag in his hand.*

RORY. Wha-hoo . . . (*He sings.*) Bags packed and all boy hah! . . . Are yeh all set, yeah?

JOSIE. Yeah.

RORY. Yeh won't know him the next time yeh see him, Terry.

TERRY. How's that?

RORY. What? They're goin' to do a bit of an exploration job on him.

TERRY. How do yeh mean?

RORY. A magical mystery tour on his innards.

TERRY. What? I thought yeh were only goin' in for a few tests.

JOSIE. Yeah well, yeh know what Thought done, don't yeh?

RORY. Yeah. He pissed in his pants and Thought he was sweatin'.

TERRY. How long will yeh be in for?

JOSIE. I don't know. A couple of weeks, I suppose.

TERRY. But sure I thought yeh were only goin' in for the mornin' – that you'd be home by dinner hour. It's a good job I didn't take any more bookin's for the group then, ain't it.

JOSIE. That's all he's worried about.

TERRY. Yeah well, it'd be nice to be told about these things like, yeh know.

JOSIE. A couple of large bottles'd go down well now.

BREDA *enters.*

BREDA. There y'are, Josie, I got those few things for yeh. (*Soap, face cloth, toothpaste, etc.*)

JOSIE. Oh right. Thanks Breda. Did yeh have enough?

BREDA. Yeah.

RORY. He has poor Breda runnin' around the place for him.

BREDA. Shut up you, and leave him alone.

RORY. Oh lord! Stop!

BREDA. God help him.

TED *returns.* JOSIE *opens up his overnight bag and puts the stuff into it.*

RORY. Do yeh know that Ted?

TED. What?

RORY. You and me don't know nothin' about women compared to this fella . . . What did yeh think of Downtown Munich last night, Breda? Queer bad weren't they?

BREDA. Oh they were alright. Sure they're only a crowd of young lads, anyway.

RORY. Yeah well, one of them became old before his time last night then, I don't mind tellin' yeh.

BREDA. Here listen, yeh know what you'll do – seein' as how we won't have Josie with us for a little while. Sing us that new song that yeh sang last night.

RORY. What?

BREDA. Go ahead . . . Wait 'til I make sure that . . . (*She goes to the door and looks across the street.*) No, I'm alright. Go on. Whatdoyoucallit . . . Sayonara Street!

RORY. Sayonara Street?

BREDA. Yeah.

RORY (*looking at his watch*). Breda!

BREDA. Never mind about that. Go ahead.

RORY. Huh?

BREDA. Go on out of that.

RORY. Is this one for real, or what, lads?

TERRY. What? I'm sure Josie is in no form for singin' now, and he just about to go into the hospital.

JOSIE. God I don't mind at all, I'll sing alright.

RORY *and* TERRY *look at one another in amazement.*

RORY. Alright, you're the boss . . . Come on, Ted, get your ass out here. (RORY *rolls back the sheet from the piano.*)

TERRY. Jaysus, if anyone sees us singin' at this hour of the day, we'll be all certified, that's all.

RORY. Not at all.

TERRY. Close over that auld door there then Rory, will yeh.

RORY. Right . . . Come on Ted, will yeh.

RORY *closes the door.* TED *comes away from the window and over to the piano.*

TED. What are we doin'? Sayonara?

TERRY. Yeah.

RORY (*to* JOSIE *while he makes a face behind* TERRY*'s back*). You make sure yeh open up your lungs boy.

JOSIE. Come on, will yez.

SONG.
> Here We Are
> It's Sayonara Street
> We've Come This Far
> And Now We Are Complete
> It's Sayonara Street
> Goodbye.
> Here We Go
> I Guess This Is The End
> Which Only Goes To Show
> That We Were More Than Friends
> You see.

> *Change.*

> On Sayonara Street
> You Know You're Alive
> You're Gazing At Your Feet
> With Tears In Your Eyes.
> Here We Are
> It's Sayonara Street
> We're Come This Far
> And Now We Are Complete
> It's Sayonara Street
> Goodbye.

> BREDA *applauds. Then she rises and goes across to give* JOSIE *a hug.*

BREDA. I'll see yeh, Josie. Look after yourself now hon, won't yeh? And listen, don't worry about it. It'll be alright.

JOSIE. Yeah, right Breda. And thanks for gettin' us the things.

BREDA. You're welcome. Have yeh a lift up to the hospital and all, yeah?

JOSIE. Yeah. Rory is givin' us a run up like, yeh know.

BREDA. Oh right. You look after him now, do yeh hear me?

RORY. Yeah right, Breda.

BREDA. And stay with him until he's checked in and all . . .
I'll come up and see yeh as soon as you're done. I'd better
run meself, or I'll be shot. I'll see yeh, Josie.

JOSIE. Yeah, see yeh Breda.

BREDA (*going*). Bye lads.

TERRY. All the best, Breda.

TED. Good luck, Breda.

RORY. See yeh, Breda.

> BREDA *is gone. A slight sad pause.*

RORY (*going for his jacket*). I left the car in the chapel yard,
Josie. I'll go and bring it around – save yeh . . .

> JOSIE *is watching* TERRY, *who is going about his work.*

JOSIE. Huh? . . . Yeah, I want to go over and get an auld paper
meself.

RORY. We never lost it all the same though lads, did we? Hah?

> *He chuckles sadly.* JOSIE *looks at the others, smiles and*
> *they leave.* TED, *who is still sitting at the piano, turns to*
> *watch him go.* TERRY *is watching* TED *all the time.*

TED. What?

TERRY. I know you've been seein' her, Ted.

TED. What?

TERRY. You're some sly boy! Yeh never said nothin' about it,
or anythin'.

TED. Yeah well, it's hardly somethin' a fella 'd want to blab
about now, is it? I mean to say . . . How did yeh find out
about it, anyway?

TERRY. She told me herself that she was seein' someone. I've
just put two and two together now.

TED. She told yeh.

TERRY. Yeah Ted, she told me . . . I had a feelin' there was somethin' on your mind this while back.

TED. Yeah? . . . And would yeh say Rory suspects anythin'?

TERRY. Rory? Why should Rory. . . Oh shit!

TED. What?

TERRY. Do you mean to tell me that you've been knockin' around with Rory's missus.

TED. Yeah. Why, who did you think it was?

TERRY. It don't matter . . . How long has this been goin' on?

TED. It started the night I went up to start the presses for her. She came over to me and . . . Well one thing led to another like, yeh know.

TERRY. How far has it gone?

TED. All the way. She's goin' to tell him tonight or tomorrow mornin' I think.

TERRY. Tell him! What does she want to tell him for? I mean what he don't know won't hurt him, will it? This'll all just blow over, and there be no real harm done. Say nothin', I say. It wasn't right what yeh done but . . . Well I mean to say, these things happen like, yeh know. Two people get thrown together like that. Well, it's only natural, ain't it?

TED. It's not goin' to blow over, Terry. I've asked her to move in with me.

TERRY. Yeh what? Are yeh mad or somethin'? Yeh can't do that.

TED. Why not?

TERRY. He's your best fuckin' friend, for fuck's sake.

TED. That don't come into it, Terry.

TERRY. Your best friend don't come into it?

TED. You don't understand, Terry. I mean to say this is not just a quick whatdoyoucallit or anythin'. I got her under my skin, yeh know – right where it hurts. When she's not around I keep wonderin' where she is and when I'm with her I don't want it to end. Yeh know. I mean what can I do?

TERRY. What can yeh do! I'll tell yeh what yeh can, Ted. Yeh can try and . . .

TED. I mean to say I've been worried sick about all of this like, yeh know . . . And I did try to stay away from her for a while and all but . . . I don't know . . .

TERRY. Don't do it, Ted. Don't do it to him. Please. You'll never have any luck if yeh do this kind of thing to your friends. Yeh know. I'm serious, Ted.

TED. Yeah well, unfortunately, so am I.

TERRY. What?

TED. Look, I don't want to be here when Rory gets back. I've been offered a bit of a tangle down the road there. I'm goin' to take my tools with me.

TERRY. What? (TERRY *watches* TED *gather up his tools.*) . . . Yeah, right Ted, you do that. Jesus! . . . (TERRY *paces up and down.*) . . . Oh Lord, Jaysus Ted! . . . Ted, Ted, Ted!

JOSIE *is standing in the doorway now.*

TED. I'll see yeh, Josie. Good luck in the hospital.

JOSIE. Yeah, see yeh Ted.

TED *takes a last look around and leaves.*

He told yeh, then?

TERRY. Can you believe that? Can yeh fuckin' well believe that? And they're supposed to be best friends.

JOSIE. Not any more, they ain't.

TERRY. Poor Rory'll be devastated about this though, yeh know. It'll break his heart, so it will.

JOSIE. Ah well, that's what friends are for, I suppose.

TERRY. Hah? . . . This'll put the kybosh on The Cavalcaders for a while too won't it? Between one thing and another, I mean.

JOSIE. I suppose.

TERRY. It's all comin' apart Josie, I think. It's all fallin' apart boy! I wouldn't mind, but I promised poor auld Eamon that I'd try and keep it all together, yeh know. But it's queer hard sometimes though, yeh know.

JOSIE. I know.

Slight pause.

TERRY. So when do yeh think they'll do yeh, then?

JOSIE. I don't know. In the mornin', I hope.

TERRY. But sure I'll come up and see yeh tonight, so. Make sure you're settled in and that . . .

JOSIE. Right. Don't forget me grapes.

TERRY. Yeah right. And I'll bring yeh up a couple of good cowboy books too – keep yeh off the nurses.

Slight pause.

JOSIE. I'll see yeh then, Terry.

TERRY. Yeah, see yeh, me auld mate. Good luck . . .

JOSIE exits. Pause. Lights down. Lights rise on the shop. Night has fallen. TERRY is alone. There is a rap on the window. TERRY goes across to open the door. He is surprised to find BREDA standing there. He invites her in.

BREDA. Did yeh get up to see Josie after?

TERRY. Yeah, I went up to see him this evenin'.

BREDA. Well, did he settle in alright, yeah?

TERRY. Yeah, he's in right form up there. Yeh should see the state of the big pyjamas on him.

BREDA. When are they doin' him?

TERRY. In the mornin', I think. Oh he'll be grand . There's a fella who don't look so hot, mind yeh – he's in the bed opposite Josie there – whatshisname, the one legged man from The Faythe. He was an insurance man.

BREDA. Oh poor Mister Kelly.

TERRY. Yeah. They had to amputate his other leg, yeh know.

BREDA. Oh God! . . . Jaysus, you'd only think you'd be bad, wouldn't yeh?

TERRY. Yeah . . .

Slight pause. TERRY *goes to her, kisses her tenderly, touches her face and hair and tries to take her in his arms. She resists, pushing him away gently.*

BREDA. Whoo . . . That's not why I'm here.

TERRY. No? . . . Sorry!

BREDA *chuckles and touches his face.*

BREDA. It's been so long since I touched yeh . . . Have yeh finished with that young one yet?

TERRY. What young one?

BREDA *throws him a dirty look.*

Oh! . . . Yeah – looks like it.

BREDA. Good.

TERRY. Is it? For who?

BREDA. For you.

TERRY *laughs.* BREDA *moves away from him.*

TERRY. Have you been seein' anyone else since?

BREDA. No . . . You're delighted, ain't yeh?

TERRY. It makes no odds to me.

BREDA. Get out of it, you'd die if yeh ever heard of me goin' with someone else. Yeh would though, Terry. That's the difference between you and me, yeh see. I don't care who you've been with before or since, as long as I end up with your name engraved on me locket. Even if yeh do write songs about other women!

TERRY. What?

BREDA. Did You See That Girl! . . . That's the first thing I'd
    have to do if I got yeh – run that bloody bank clerk out of
    town.

TERRY. That song wasn't written about her.

BREDA. Oh yeah, pull the other one Terry.

TERRY. I'm tellin' yeh it wasn't. It was about you. (BREDA
    scoffs.) . . . I'm tellin' yeh . . . I was here all by meself right,
    tryin' to think of somethin' to write about. I went to the
    window – half hopin' I'll admit to see Beautiful Bundoran
    goin' by but there was no sign of her. Anyway the next
    thing you came out of the hairdressers and I saw yeh goin'
    down the street, with your little slender neck on yeh and all,
    and your raincoat clingin' into your body when yeh walked.
    And then yeh said hello to someone, and I knew straight
    away that this street belonged to you, that no one else could
    compare to yeh – not around here anyway. So I wrote the
    song.

He sings softly.

    . . . Hey Mister. Did You See That Girl. She Walks Around
    Like She Owned The World. You'd Think She Owned The
    World . . .

BREDA. Yeh always were a lovely liar, Terry.

TERRY. Huh?

BREDA. What's wrong with yeh, Terry?

TERRY. How do yeh mean?

BREDA. Well, you're goin' around the place there – I don't
    know – runnin' away all the time. I mean what the hell's
    wrong with yeh at all, eh? You're like a fella who's
    just waitin' for somethin' better to come along or some-
    thin'. Nothin' better is goin' to come along Terry. I'm
    the best you're goin' to do boy! Resign yourself to it!
    (*He chuckles*.) . . . I mean what is it you're supposed to be
    waitin' for anyway?

TERRY. Oh I don't know Breda. . . . Sometimes I think I'm
    just waitin' for him to come back and tell me that he's sorry

or somethin', yeh know. Childish I know but there yeh go . . .
I always knew that he'd take her from me, yeh know –
eventually. Well I always knew he could if he wanted to,
let's put it that way . . . I never had any peace with her.
Right from the word go. I was always wonderin' where she
was and who she was with, and what she was up to, and all
the rest of it. I mean it wasn't all Rogan's fault or anythin'.
Not really! . . . Then one rainy Sunday afternoon shortly
after we were married she went missin' for a few hours.
I nearly went frantic lookin' for her – down the auld side
streets and alleyways I went – walkin' around for hours in
the rain. Nearly drove meself doolally I did . . . I went home
then only to discover that she was already there before me –
the table set, the tea ready. She'd been to her mother's.
I could have kicked meself. Until I saw her pluck a bit of
moss from the hem of her dress.

Silence.

BREDA. He was never a patch on you, Terry.

TERRY. Yeah, that's why he ended up with the rose and me
with the thorn.

BREDA. Thanks very much.

TERRY. What? (*He chuckles sadly and touches her hand
tenderly.*) I never knew you fancied Jacques?

BREDA. The other way round, yeh mean.

TERRY. Yeah?

BREDA. Don't sound so surprised Terry. It could happen, yeh
know.

He laughs.

BREDA. I used to love lookin' at you, yeh know. I used to
make plans to kidnap yeh and everything . . . I'd give
anything to be able to turn back the clock for yeh, Terry, to
turn yeh back into the lovely fella yeh used to be that time.
Where did he go to at all, eh?

*She touches his face, kisses him gently and leaves. Lights
down. Lights rise.* TERRY *is dressed in his heavy overcoat.*

RORY *enters from the back room and goes behind the counter to put the kettle on.*

RORY. We' ll have a cup of tea I think . . . Are yeh alright, Terry?

TERRY. Yeah. A bit hot, that's all.

RORY. What? Jaysus you're boilin' up there. Are yeh OK?

TERRY. Yeah, I'm alright.

RORY *bends down and picks up a cardboard box full of stuff from the floor – old newspapers and photographs, etc. He puts it on the counter.*

RORY. There's a feckin' rake of stuff here, yeh know. All the auld music sheets though, hah? And Eamon's auld tunin' fork.

TERRY. What?

RORY. Look at this! . . . (*Reading from an old newspaper.*) FREAK STORM ROCKS THE WOODENWORKS. 'A freak storm rocked the Woodenworks and devastated the quayside last Friday night when heavy waves pounded the waterfront and the surrounding area.' Look at the size of those waves, Terry. That's a great picture ain't it? Hah? (*He finds an old newspaper cutting.*) YOUNG WOMAN PLUNGES TO HER DEATH! 'A young woman plunged from the bridge into the water last Friday night. Eye witnesses said that they could hear the young woman cry out for help before she hit the water but the high winds and heavy seas hampered her rescue and she was tragically drowned . . . That was the queer one who used to work over in the little corner shop here, Terry. I heard after that she was knockin' around with your man Poe the undertaker, yeh know. They say she was pregnant for him and he dumped her. And he a Confraternity man too, hah! (*He chuckles.*) . . . Jaysus she got an awful death after – the poor crator anyway!

NUALA *appears in the back room doorway and there is something chilling about her appearance.* TERRY *turns to look at her. She is invisible to* RORY *throughout the scene.*

But sure, that girl wasn't right in the head anyway like, yeh know. She was a bit airy I think, wasn't she?

NUALA *comes towards* TERRY.

NUALA. He's alright there, of course . . . With his black suit and his big black coat and his pioneer badge and his fáinne and his black diamond on his arm and all the rest of it. Well maybe he won't feel so tall when I spill the beans on him. Maybe he won't look so sure of himself then.

TERRY. You say nothin'. That man is a married man with a family.

NUALA. So?

TERRY. You knew that before yeh started foolin' around with him. Now take your punishment and stop whingin'.

NUALA. So I'm the one who has to pay the piper while he gets away scot free is that it?

TERRY. Are you on somethin', or what?

NUALA. What?

TERRY. Did you take somethin'? Nuala, did you take somethin', I said.

NUALA. Yeah. A spoonful of sugar . . . (*She laughs.*)

TERRY. What?

NUALA. I think I'm in trouble, Terry.

TERRY. What do yeh mean?

NUALA. And there's an auld fog comin' down around me too, yeh know.

TERRY. What do yeh mean, you're in trouble?

NUALA. Sometimes I find meself lookin' into a sort of a two-way mirror. I'm sort of on the inside, yeh know – lookin' out at meself.

TERRY. Nuala, what do yeh mean, you're in trouble?

NUALA. Sometimes I look into the mirror and there's no reflection there at all. No shadow either. I go around the place lookin' behind me all the time lookin' for a shadow.

It's as if I don't really exist at all, yeh know . . . He used to beat me, yeh know. With his belt. Down in the cellar below his shop. Do you think I bring out the worst in men, Terry? (*She smiles manically.*)

TERRY. What?

NUALA. He told me I was like Eve. He said that Eve came into the Garden and ruined everything. Take me back Terry, please. Let's start again . . .

TERRY. No way.

NUALA. It's a terrible lousy thing to do, yeh know Terry – to take somebody's love and throw it back in their face like that.

TERRY. I never took your love.

NUALA. It's a queer lousy thing to do boy.

TERRY. I never took your love. I never said anythin' about love.

NUALA. If you don't take me back I swear I'll throw meself off of the bridge or somethin'.

TERRY. Now don't start that, Nuala. Yeh know that kind of talk gets on my wick. Anyway you made your bed the night yeh chose him instead of me.

NUALA. You told me to.

TERRY. I what?

NUALA. You said you were only usin' me. You told me to.

TERRY. I told yeh to! Get the fuck out of here, will yeh! I told yeh to!

NUALA *falls to her knees and wraps her arms around* TERRY*'s legs, clinging to him in desperation.*

NUALA. Please Terry, take me back. I promise yeh I'll do anythin' yeh want. I swear . . .

TERRY. Come up out of it, will yeh. Stop haulin' out of me! Come up I said. Stand up. Get up. Look at yeh. Look, there's your shadow there behind yeh. And there's mine.

Yours is young and mine is old. I'm old and you're young.
Get it? Got it? Good! Now hold on to it.

NUALA. If you don't take me back I'm goin' to throw meself
off the bridge, yeh know.

TERRY. Throw yourself off the bridge! You wouldn't have the
nerve to throw yourself off that counter there. Yeh haven't
even got the guts to look at yourself in the mirror, let alone
throw yourself off the bridge.

NUALA. I will. I'll do it. I'll show the lot of yeh. I'll show
you. I'll show him too. Because you're nothin' only a pair
of lousers, Terry. Dirty lousers yeh are, the pair of yeh. (*She
is backing her way towards the door.*)

TERRY. Nuala.

NUALA. It's a terrible lousy thing to do, yeh know. I mean to
say yeh take somebody's love and throw it back in their face
like that . . . I'll do it. I swear to God, I'll do it . . .

TERRY. Nuala.

She turns and flees.

Nuala . . .

TED *and* JOSIE *enter from the back room in high spirits.*
TED *goes to the piano and they launch into 'Genevieve',
barber shop style.*

TERRY. Nuala . . . Nuala . . . Nuala . . .

TERRY *turns to find* TED *sitting at the piano.* RORY *is at
his side.* JOSIE *is in his usual place, sitting on the edge of
the piano.* TED *and* JOSIE *are in their stage suits. They
have drifted into 'Now Is The Hour'.* TERRY*'s face lights
up at the sight and sound of them. He joins in with the
singing, his hands outstretched.*

RORY. Hey Terry, these two fellas wore their suits into the
pub, yeh know.

SONG. Soon I'll Return To Find

You Waiting Here . . .

TERRY. Oon the lads. All me auld mates, hah.

TED *goes into a 'I Say I Say I Say' routine on the piano.*

JOSIE. I say I say I say. Did you hear about the man who tried to poison his wife with a razor blade. He gave her arse an nick.

RORY. I say I say I say. Did you hear about the three hens?

JOSIE and TERRY. The Three Hens?

RORY. Yes, the Three Hens. One was normal, one was dyslexic and the third was a nymphomaniac. The first one said 'cocka doodle doo,' the second said, 'doodle doodle cock', and the third said, 'any cock'll doo.'

JOSIE and TERRY (*sing*). I am a Westmeath Bachelor and my age is twenty-three.

TERRY. I say I say I say. Any news on the budget?

JOSIE. The budget? Ah yes, I do believe that aeroplanes are going up, submarines are going down, while envelopes and notepaper remain stationary.

ALL (*sing*) And That's Why I'm A Bachelor And I Don't Intend To Wed.

They laugh.

TED. Did yeh see the state of the auld caretaker when he heard us doin' the 'any cock'll do' joke. He nearly jawlocked himself laughin', that's all.

RORY. And did yeh see the big bunch of keys he had on him? It's a wonder he didn't do himself a mischief liftin' them.

JOSIE. Yeah, some dirty get laced the poor man's tea with whisky too, though.

RORY. Yeah I wonder who that was now?

JOSIE. Hey boy, don't look at me.

TED. Did yeh see him goin' down the stairs. He was like a puppet. Happy New Year says he!

JOSIE (*tearful with laughter*). He was absolutely footless wasn't he? Oh dear, oh dear . . .

TERRY. All the boys, hah! And Josie, me auld mate!

JOSIE. What . . . (JOSIE*'s expression changes as they embrace.*) Your uncle Eamon knows, Terry. She's after tellin' him I think.

TERRY. What?

JOSIE. He knows. She told him.

TERRY. When?

JOSIE. She told him, I'm tellin' yeh . . . (JOSIE *breaks away, turns to* TED *and* RORY.) . . . Yeah, Eamon's missus. She took the pair of us on in the back room there.

RORY. Yeah?

JOSIE. We were only young fellas at the time now. I mean to say, we didn't know any better or anythin'. But she was lyin' up on the auld table inside there. Terry went into her first and then when he came out, she called me in.

RORY. Jaysus she must have been mad for it, was she?

JOSIE. Oh stop! Although she was sort of cryin' when I went in though, like, yeh know.

RORY. Yeah? . . . Jaysus hah!

TED *begins to play The Alleluia from Eamon's mass.*

TERRY. Are yeh sure she told him Josie? Where's me uncle now, Josie? . . . Josie . . . Jesus . . .

BREDA (*enters*). Are you fellas comin' over to the dance, or what?

TED. What? Yeah right Breda.

JOSIE. New Year's Eve, Breda, 1968!

BREDA. What about it?

JOSIE. Jacques LePouvier kissed Marian Noakes and what happened?

BREDA. I don't know, tell me, what happened?

JOSIE. She blossomed! Right or wrong? And this was a one with neither shape nor make to her now. New Year's Eve, right. Jacques goes over, takes her in his arms and boom.

Her whole face lit up, boy I'm not coddin' yeh. Two weeks later Dinky Doyle is tellin' me that he's after fallin' in love with her – a girl he wouldn't even look at the summer before. Marvellous too what can happen though, ain't it? Hah? The face of Breda!

BREDA. The face of you, yeh mean!

JOSIE. What?

BREDA. Go away from me, will yeh, and come on.

JOSIE. What?

BREDA *leaves. The others make to follow.* JOSIE *laughs, eyes to heaven.*

Oh Marian Noakes, where are yeh now?

The others laugh. TED *and* JOSIE *leave.* TERRY *stands to watch them go. A choir is singing the Alleluia, heard only by* TERRY. *He basks in it, tears in his eyes.* RORY *comes up behind him.*

RORY. Are yeh alright, Terry?

TERRY. What? Yeah.

RORY. The only thing is worryin' me now is how the hell we're goin' to get this auld piano out the door here. I mean I know technically speaking if it went in, then it should come out. But how? . . . How did they get it in here, anyway?

TERRY. What? The piano?

RORY. Yeah.

TERRY. They had an awful job, sure. The whole street was out pushin' and shovin'. And that came out of our little kitchen, yeh know. An awful weight in it, too. In the end they had to take down the doorframe and everything and big Tom Nail the coalman told everyone to stand aside while he pushed it through sideways through the hole in the wall. Meself and Josie were only little lads that time and I was killed tryin' to look inside the piano because someone told me that there was a man's name carved under the lid somewhere It was great to hear Eamon's Mass sung at Josie's funeral that time though, wasn't it?

RORY. What?

TERRY. Josie's brother asked me to sit in with the family, yeh
    know It was queer nice of him boy! And later on I helped to
    carry the coffin with them. Poor auld Josie though hah! . . .
    A spoonful of sugar, says she!

RORY. Who? (TERRY *looks at him vacantly.*)

   RORY *looks at* TERRY, *a little concerned about him. He
   goes across to the counter. He leafs through an old dusty
   child's copy book which he leaves on the counter. He picks
   up an old photograph.*

   There's a great photo. Who is it? There's you, anyway.
   And Josie. Josie didn't change a bit did he? And who's that
   lad? . . . He looks like Billy Fury, don't he?

TERRY. What?

   TERRY *looks at the photo.* RORY *goes back to the counter
   for the box.*

RORY. I'll leave this auld box over the bench for yeh, Terry,
    just in case you're wanting anything out of it or anything.

TERRY. Yeah, right, Rory. Thanks.

RORY. I'm goin' to tell yeh one thing though, me auld son, but
    you're one sound man boy!

TERRY. What? . . . I've done some queer things in me time
    though Rory, yeh know. I mean I've a lot to answer for.

RORY. Show me the man that hasn't.

   RORY *lays the cardboard down on the bench and goes back
   in behind the counter.* TERRY *sits on the bench and takes
   from the box a sprig of mistletoe. He titters.*

RORY. What?

TERRY. Mistletoe, be Jaysus!

RORY. What? Yeah.

   TERRY *loses himself in thought. We hear music far off in
   the distance, a corny band playing The Conga.* RORY *is
   oblivious to it until* JOSIE *and* BREDA *and* TED *and*

NUALA *come dancing in with party hats on their heads,*

JOSIE. Happy New Year! . . . (*To* TERRY.) Happy New Year, me auld son.

BREDA (*breaks away to kiss him*). Happy New Year, Terry.

TERRY*'s face is aglow as they all dance into the back room and back out again,* RORY *joining them.*

JOSIE. Happy New Year!

JOSIE *snakes them in behind the counter and then back into the back room again,* NUALA *staying behind, a little breathless.*

NUALA. I'm Nuala. I work in the shop across the street.

TERRY. I know. I often saw yeh goin' in and out. I'm Terry.

NUALA. Happy New Year, Terry.

TERRY. The same to you.

NUALA *smiles and eyes the mistletoe in his hand.*

It's a shame to waste it.

NUALA. What?

TERRY *goes to her and kisses her gently. She looks into his eyes and sighs. He kisses her again and she responds to him. He touches her face and studies it etc as she basks in the nearness of him.*

NUALA (*cooing beneath his touch*). Mmn . . .

The others return. TERRY *and* NUALA *break away from one another.* BREDA, *full of festive glee, dances with* JOSIE *through the shop and out onto the street.*

TED. What do yeh mean? We go every year, don't we?

RORY. Not this year, I'm afraid.

TED. Why not?

RORY. Because Ursula is up in the house on her own with the baby and . . .

TED. Ursula, Ursula,Ursula! You'd give anyone the shits talkin' about Ursula.

RORY. What's that supposed to mean?

TED. Ah.

RORY. I mean it's alright for you, Ted.

TED. Why, because I'm not tied to the apron strings, yeh mean.

RORY. No, because you're nothin', only a lonely bottle with no one belongin' to yeh.

TED. I have plenty of fella to drink with, mate. And I can get a woman anytime I feel like it.

RORY. Yeah sure.

TED. What do yeh mean, yeah sure.

RORY. Yeah sure – yeh can get a woman anytime yeh feel like it.

TED. What?

JOSIE (*returns*). What's wrong with the two of you, eh?

TED (*exits*). He's makin' out.

RORY (*off*). Makin' out? What am I supposed to be makin' out?

TED (*off*). You're makin' out that I'm a whatdoyoucallit . . .

RORY (*off*). Will you go and cop on to yourself Ted . . .

NUALA. I can see yeh workin' from my window, yeh know.

TERRY. Can yeh?

NUALA. Yeah. And the other day I heard yeh singin'.

TERRY. What was I singin'?

NUALA. I don't know. Somethin' about the moon.

TERRY. Somethin' about the moon? It could have been anythin'.

NUALA. I know.

TERRY *chuckles and kisses her again.* JOSIE *turns to look at them.*

JOSIE. Your uncle Eamon's in a pretty bad way over there, Terry. I think maybe you should go over to him . . . Terry.

TERRY (*entranced by the girl*). What?

JOSIE. I say I think maybe you should go over to him. I think she's after tellin' him, yeh know.

TERRY. Yeah.

BREDA (*entering*). Josie, come out here quick will yeh, before these two fellas kill one another out here.

JOSIE. What? What's up?

BREDA. Come on, they're killin' one another out here. (JOSIE *goes*.) . . . They should be ashamed of themselves, two friends fightin' like that on New Year's Eve . . . Are you comin' back to the dance or what Nuala?

NUALA. What? Yeah . . . Are you comin' over?

TERRY. I'll be over in a minute.

NUALA *smiles and follows* BREDA *out the door.*

Music dies. TERRY *chuckles to himself.* RORY *enters from the back room. The music in the distance fades to nothing.*

RORY. What?

TERRY. Nothin'.

RORY. Terry smilin' away to himself there . . . Did yeh see the cups anyway? . . . the place is in an uproar boy . . . When the sheets are shorter the beds look longer, hah! I don't know!

RORY *takes two dusty mugs and goes out to the back room again.* TERRY *tosses the sprig of mistletoe into the box again. He sits. Suddenly* JOSIE *appears in the doorway again, a party hat on his head.*

JOSIE. She's after tellin' him alright. Terry.

TERRY. What? When?

JOSIE. At the stroke of midnight. She's some bitch, boy! Poor auld Eamon is in an awful way over there!

TERRY. Why though? I mean it was so long ago!

NUALA *is standing in the back room doorway, laughing.*
TERRY *turns to her.*

What?

NUALA. It was probably the first and last time for Josie.

TERRY *laughs. He turns to find that* JOSIE *is gone and then turns to discover that* BREDA *is standing where* NUALA *used to be. He frowns and begins pacing the room.*

BREDA. I was only dancin' with him, Terry.

TERRY. Yeh danced nearly every second dance with him, is what I heard.

BREDA. Yeah well, that's why I go down there like – to dance. It's Ballroom Dancin' like, yeh know, and he's sort of my partner. He's a good dancer .

TERRY. I thought Dinky was supposed to be your partner?

BREDA. We changed round. Your man Poe is sort of my partner now.

TERRY. What way did he hold yeh?

BREDA. What? Normal.

TERRY. Show me.

BREDA. He sort of held me like this . . .

TERRY. Show me, I said.

BREDA. What? . . . (*She takes* TERRY*'s arm and guides it around her body.*) . . . He put one arm around me like that and he held my hand in his like that. Yeh know. Just normal!

TERRY. Are yeh sure it wasn't like this?

He draws her roughly towards him. Disappointed, she frees herself from his grip. Pause. He begins to pace again, slightly angry.

How did Josie get on?

BREDA. Good. He sounds good, yeh know – with the orchestra behind him and all. He looks good too . . . But sure you should come down there some night, Terry. You're a lovely dancer. And it's a right bit of laugh, yeh know. That's all it is Terry – a bit of laugh!

TERRY. Yeah?

He looks at her, full of uncertainty. She nods sadly.

BREDA. . . . What's wrong with yeh?

TERRY. I don't know. I'm beginnin' to care about where yeh go and who you're with, and all the rest of it. I don't like it.

BREDA. But sure that's good ain't it? That yeh care!

TERRY. I'm not so sure about that.

Slight pause.

BREDA. Yeah well, that's not why I'm here anyway. I need to talk to yeh about somethin' else.

TERRY. What?

She throws him a dirty look.

BREDA. I'm gettin' tired of it Terry – all this cloak and dagger stuff. I mean I'm tired sneakin' round in the dark all the time, yeh know. I want it all out in the open now.

TERRY. How do yeh mean?

BREDA. It's time we settled down Terry – you and me. Yeh know. I mean . . . Don't yeh think it's time we settled down?

TERRY. I've been down that road once before, Breda.

BREDA. Not with me, yeh haven't.

TERRY. No one was supposed to fall, Breda. We agreed. No strings attached. That's what we said.

BREDA. You said, yeh mean.

TERRY. But sure I thought yeh said yeh liked comin' over here anyway? . . . So what is this, an ultimatum or somethin'?

BREDA. Call it what yeh like. But I'm not comin' over here again – not like this anyway. If you want to see me again you can call over to the house for me. Ask me out properly – on a proper date. Take me somewhere nice.

TERRY(*pacing*). Jesus!

BREDA. Will yeh do that for me?

TERRY. I don't know, we'll see.

BREDA (*disappointed*). Oh!

TERRY. Now don't get all stroppy on me. We'll see, I said.
Yeh know . . . I mean . . . We'll see.

BREDA. OK. . . . I'll see yeh then, Terry.

TERRY. Yeah right Breda, see yeh.

> BREDA *turns to leave. She stops in the doorway to look at
> him.*

BREDA. Jaysus, Terry!

> *Slight pause. She leaves sadly. The sound of music as* JOSIE
> *appears, dressed in a beautiful white dinner jacket etc. He
> looks really handsome. He steps up to a microphone and
> sings, 'Smoke Gets In Your Eyes'.* NUALA *is standing in
> the back room doorway, smiling.* TERRY *looks at her
> tenderly. He goes to her and takes her in his arms. They
> dance. They continue to dance when the song ends, their
> dancing feet shuffling like a played out record.* JOSIE *is gone.*

NUALA. Breda wants me to go Ballroom Dancing with her,
yeh know.

TERRY. Does she?

NUALA. Yeah. Do yeh think I should?

TERRY. If yeh like.

NUALA. Would yeh mind?

> TERRY *shakes his head.* NUALA *smiles at him tenderly.*

Listen, I'm wantin' you to come over and see my little room
sometime . . . Will yeh?

TERRY. OK.

NUALA. I'll read yeh some of my poetry by candlelight. And
I'll light a big fire and we'll lie down on the mat together.
Will yeh come over though? (TERRY *nods.*) . . . When?

TERRY. Soon.

NUALA. That's good. You'd better, now. I love being with
you, Terry, yeh know. I swear the whole world stops turnin'
when you're inside of me. And everything goes real quiet.
So so silent! All I can hear is the sound of my heart beatin'.
And the sound of my own . . . ecstasy . . . I love hearin'
about your exploits with all those other women too –
where yeh took them and how it all came about and that.
Sometimes I pretend to be standin' in their shoes as they
come to you. Other times I imagine I'm you waitin' for
them to come to me. Like the one about your lovely
neighbour with the big bottom who rides her bike past your
house every day. And when she came to sell you a raffle
ticket or something you asked her in and yeh stripped her
naked in the parlour, and yeh told her to stand up on a chair
so that you could have a good look at her, and that. I love
hearin' that one . . . (TERRY *laughs*.) What?

TERRY. I only made that one up.

NUALA. Yeh what? Yeh didn't . . . Ah yeh didn't . . . That's
my favourite one!

TERRY. I know.

NUALA. Yeh didn't though really, did yeh . . . Ah no, that's
not fair. (*She hits him playfully*.)

TERRY. What?

NUALA. How many of the others did yeh make up?

TERRY. Hah?

NUALA. I bet yeh made them all up. You were probably never
with another woman in your life.

TERRY. Hey. (*He presents himself*.)

She laughs and kisses him. He draws her in close to him.

NUALA. Yes Terry. Yes. Yes . . .

TERRY. We can't. The boys'll be arrivin' soon.

NUALA. Get rid of them.

TERRY. What?

NUALA. Lock the door. Draw the blinds. Turn out the lights.

TERRY. We can't. Yeh know we can't . . . Anyway I'm all washed out.

NUALA. What –

TERRY. I'm bet. You win.

NUALA. Do yeh give up?

TERRY. Yeah. I give up.

She chuckles and looks deep into his eyes.

NUALA. They say you can fall in love with anybody, yeh know. All yeh need is time. But I don't believe that. I believe in fate. And destiny. I believe that you end up where you belong . . . I hope so anyway . . . (*She frowns.*)

TERRY. What's wrong?

NUALA. Sometimes I feel a bit ashamed of the things I ask you to do to me.

TERRY. Why?

NUALA. I don't know. I just do.

TERRY. There's no need to be.

NUALA. I know but . . .

TERRY. . . . Look, I told yeh before, I'd do anything yeh want me to do. As long as yeh don't ask me to hurt yeh or anythin'.

NUALA. You'll probably do that anyway Terry – in time.

Slight pause.

TERRY. You'd better be goin', Nuala.

NUALA. OK . . . When will I see you again?

TERRY. Tomorrow sometime.

NUALA. I love you Terry . . . Did yeh hear me?

TERRY *nods.*

TERRY. Go ahead.

NUALA. OK. . . . Bye.

NUALA *leaves softly. Slight pause.* RORY *enters with the washed mugs.*

RORY. Yeh know I'm nearly sure I saw a man's name somewhere inside that auld piano one time . . . Wait 'til I have a look see . . . I believe the other one is pregnant again too, yeh know.

TERRY. Who's that?

RORY. Ursula. I saw herself and Ted goin' by there just the other day. I wasn't talkin' to them or anythin'. I just said hello to them and that . . .

TERRY. Yeah?

RORY *is on his belly now, looking inside the piano.*

RORY. All water under the bridge now, Terry. I don't know where this is. I'm nearly sure I . . .

JOSIE *enters, dressed in pyjamas and dressing-gown etc.*

JOSIE. How's it goin', me auld son?

TERRY (*rises, delighted*). Josie!

JOSIE. I see poor auld Kelly in there without a leg to stand on, hah!

TERRY. Yeah.

JOSIE. Thanks for the grapes. (TERRY *nods.*) . . . Thanks for the rabbit says she, the soup was gorgeous. Do yeh miss me?

TERRY. Yeah, I do.

JOSIE. Hah? (*He smiles and sings.*) Heart Of My Heart. I Love That Melody. Too Bad We Had To Part. (TERRY *sings along with him, sadly harmonising.*) I Know A Tear Would Glisten. If Once More I Could Listen. To That Gang That Sang. Heart Of My Heart. (*He chuckles.*) . . .

JOSIE. Jaysus it's gas though too, Terry ain't it, when yeh think of it? Hah? . . . I mean you regret somethin' yeh did a long long time ago and here am I sort of ashamed of somethin' I never done at all . . . But she was sort of cryin' when I went into her though, yeh know. I mean the woman was cryin' for Jaysus sake. Yeh know?

Slight pause. He leaves.

RORY. I was right. Here it is here, look. R. Deacon . . . Sounds like a Protestant name don't it? Or Anglo-Irish or somethin'. A whatdoyoucallit – an aristocratic piano tuner hah! –

During the next speech NUALA *appears in the back room doorway.*

RORY. You can just picture him though, can't yeh? Goin' from town to town. A little hat on his head, his tools in a bag. Like a doctor! And one of those brown shop coats on him. An auld tunin' fork stickin' up out of his top pocket. He probably stayed down in The White Horse Inn or some-where – rising up every mornin' to try and drum up a bit of business. The Tate School or the Confraternity Band room or somewhere. Or some auld workingman's club maybe. Mister R. Deacon hah! February 1947! (*He chuckles sadly and puts the piano back together etc.* NUALA *smiles a forgiving smile and leaves.* BREDA *enters.*) Congratulations Breda!

BREDA. Why, what did I do now?

RORY. You've just inherited a piano.

BREDA. Oh no, that one there?

RORY. Yeah.

BREDA (*to* TERRY). Well it's goin' up in the attic. I'm not havin' that in me livin' room . . . Do yeh hear me? He's been threatenin' to have the attic converted this six months or more and he still hasn't got around to it. Are yeh alright?

RORY. He's burnin' up there, so he is.

BREDA. What? . . . He is too. What's wrong with yeh?

TERRY. I'm not well.

BREDA. Aw! Yeh poor crator yeh. Come on, I'll get yeh home to bed. There's a terrible dose goin' around though, yeh know. He's burnin' up there . . . But sure, I suppose that's way out of tune and everythin', is it?

TERRY. No, it's not too bad, mind yeh. (*He crosses to the piano.*)

BREDA. What? How are things, Rory?

RORY. Alright.

BREDA. Are yeh all set?

RORY. Just about. Yeh won't know the place the next time yeh see it, Breda.

BREDA. Yeah? Big plans hah?

RORY. Oh yeah. New counter along here, a bench out there and bare floorboards out to the door all varnished and all.

BREDA. Lovely. It sounds lovely anyway.

TERRY *is playing, 'One Heart Broken', on the piano.*

RORY. The Cavalcaders, hah! Take a look in that auld cardboard box there, Breda. Your whole life'll flash before yeh girl. (BREDA *goes to the box and plucks from it the old newspaper.*) That's a great picture, Breda, ain't it? Freak Storm Rocks The Woodenworks hah!

BREDA. Mmn . . . That was the night you came knockin' on my door wasn't it? He was afraid of the dark, weren't yeh? (*She goes to him.*)

TERRY (*nods*). That was before I got lucky.

BREDA. Aw! (*She hugs and kisses him.*)

TERRY. How did your dancin' go after?

BREDA. Alright. Little Dinky nearly danced the legs off of me that's all. (*She sings.*) Jealousy. Da Da Da Da Da Da Da . . . Did yeh ever see him dancin', Rory?

RORY. Who's that?

BREDA. Little Dinky Doyle. He's a lovely dancer. I'm tryin' to get this fella to come down but he won't budge at all.

RORY. Why not?

TERRY. I'm bad enough now.

BREDA. It's a right bit of laugh down there though, yeh know. All the auld songs an' all . . .

RORY (*reading from a dusty child's copy book*). Oh Rowan Tree, Oh Rowan Tree, Oh Won't You Tell Me. Why Do the

Wind Not Blow Through Your Leaves? And Why Do I Feel
So Safe In Your Breast? Oh Rowan Tree, Oh Rowan Tree,
Why Are You So Blessed?

RORY *shakes his head and chuckles.* TERRY *buries his
head into his hands.*

BREDA. Listen, come on. I'll get you home to bed. I'll see
yeh, Rory.

RORY. Yeah right, lads.

BREDA. And listen, good luck with everything. And don't
forget if yeh ever need anything now, yeh know where we
are. Tell him.

TERRY. Oh sure he knows that. All he has to do is shout.

BREDA. Do yeh hear that?

RORY. Yeah. Thanks very much.

BREDA *gives her little wave.*

TERRY. I'll see yeh in the mornin' sometime, Rory.

BREDA. No yeh won't. You won't be seein' anyone for a few
days – until yeh shake off that auld flu or whatever it is yeh
have.

TERRY. That's what I've to put up with now, Rory.

BREDA. It's a pity about him, Rory, ain't it? Hah? Come on.
Bye hon.

RORY. Yeah, see yeh, lads.

TERRY. I wonder if there's any pictures of Beautiful Bundoran
in that auld box.

BREDA. Come on. I'll Beautiful Bundoran yeh.

TERRY What? I'll see yeh, Rory.

TERRY *winks at* RORY. *They leave. Pause.* RORY *puts the
light out and leaves. Pause. Lights down.*

I'm Leaning on the Lamppost

Alleluia

One Heart Broken

That Girl

Sayonara Street

Genevieve

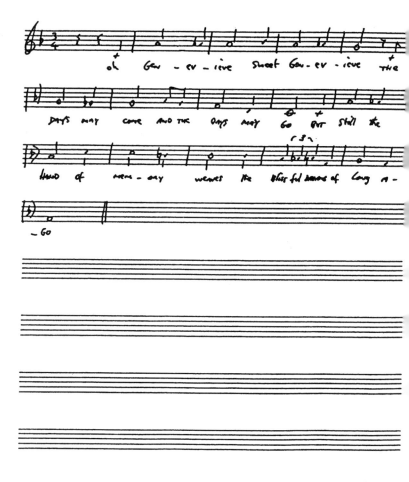

Now is the Hour

AMPHIBIANS

for Gerry

Amphibians was first presented in its original version by the
Royal Shakespeare Company at the Barbican Pit in London
on 3 September 1992. The cast was as follows:

BROADERS	Sean Murray
HUMPY	Lalor Roddy
ISAAC	KevinBurke
ZAK	Barry Lynch
SONIA	Lesley McGuire
VERONICA	Jane Gurnett
BRIDIE	Hilary Cromie
DRIBBLER	Albie Woodington
BRIAN	Richard Bonneville
MOSEY	Liam O'Callaghan
EAGLE	Ian McElhinney

Directed by Michael Attenborough
Designed by Michael Taylor

Amphibians was first presented in this revised version at
Y.M.C.A., Wexford on 1 June 1998. The cast was as follows:

BROADERS	Gary Lydon/Paul O'Brian
HUMPY	David Ganly/Brian Doherty
ISAAC	Dermot Murphy
ZAK	Claude Clancy
SONIA	Aileen Donohue
VERONICA	Brid Malone
BRIDIE	Maureen Mythen
DRIBBLER	Billy Roche
BRIAN	Steven Murphy
MOSEY	Oliver Sinnott
EAGLE	Stanley Townsend

Directed by Billy Roche
Designed by David Redmond

Setting

For the First Act, the stage is divided into sections.

*The main stage-setting is the space that leads up to the
Menapia Seafood Factory. The gates of the factory are situated
against the back wall. Nets and ropes and barrels and rusty
old lobster pots etc., are strewn in the weeds that flourish all
around. Outside the gates, which is the main acting area,
heaps of mussel sacks are piled in various groups on the
ground or stacked on the hand trolley that is used to take them
into the factory. A water barrel stands close by and a glowing
brazier. A crumbling wall looks down onto the sea and behind
the gates we can see an old dilapidated boat which is cluttered
with wellington boots, wooden crates and a rusty tar can, etc.*

*The second section is the kitchen, perhaps mounted on a raised
dais, surrounded by mussel sacks and bleeding into the set.
A back-door leads out into the little yard.*

*Downstage right, a little overgrown graveyard nestles beneath
a gnarled old tree.*

*For the Second Act, the factory gates and the mussel sacks,
etc., are cleared to become Useless Island, a deserted but
strangely enchanted island that lies a few miles from the shore.
A hut is built with wooden pilings that are lashed together with
rope and sheets of plywood nailed to the sides, and the whole
lot is covered with tarpaulin.*

*The little graveyard remains throughout as does the kitchen
and yard.*

Characters

BROADERS
HUMPY O'BRIEN
ZAK
VERONICA
ISAAC
SONIA
EAGLE
DRIBBLER
BRIDIE
MOSEY
BRIAN TAYLOR

The play is set in the present in Wexford, a small town in Ireland.

ACT ONE

Darkness, BRIDIE'*s voice sings.*

> I let my hair down
> I slipped my shoes off,
> Danced like an angel
> But I still didn't win his heart.
> Leaves of a willow
> Under my pillow,
> Calling him softly
> As I slumbered . . .

> *The lights rise. Early morning, we are outside the factory
> gates.* BROADERS *is kneeling beside a glowing brazier,
> heating up the blade of his knife.* ZAK *and* HUMPY *are
> close by. A night watchman's light glimmers.*

BROADERS. Yes, it's reddenin' up nicely Humpy.

HUMPY. What's that?

BROADERS. I say it won't be long more now, boy!

> *Slight pause.*

HUMPY. What are yeh lookin' at, Zak?

ZAK. Your man divin' off the shelter wall there.

HUMPY. Oh yeah. Did yeh see that Broaders? The fella in the
office is divin' off the shelter wall. He has all the gear on
him look – flippers and frogsuit and all boy. He's divin'
down around there this past few days, yeh know . . . Cute
enough too, ain't he? You'd never know what you'd find
down there, boy.

ZAK. Go away, there'd be nothin' worth talkin' about down
there.

HUMPY. I don't know Zak! Yeh never know! But sure he
pulled a rake of stuff out of there the other day.

BROADERS. Someone should tell that fella to leave things where they fall.

HUMPY. He's queer and spooky lookin' from here though Zak, ain't he? Whist, the Lonesome Boatman is on the horizon lads.

ZAK. Hah.

HUMPY. Eagle . . . on his way home there. Do yeh see him? With a boat full of nothin', hah! He was out for about seventeen hours or somethin' the other day there, Broaders, I heard, and all he caught was his death of cold.

ZAK. Well, at least he's a tryer, yeh have to give him that.

BROADERS. Yes! (*The Blade.*)

HUMPY. Do yeh hear that, Broaders? Eagle's a tryer according to Zak.

BROADERS. Start rollin' up your sleeve there, Humpy.

HUMPY. What?

BROADERS. You heard me.

HUMPY. Ah, no Broaders, that's not fair now. That looks redder to me that it was for any of the rest of yez.

BROADERS. Look, just roll up your sleeve there and stop actin' the babby all the time.

HUMPY. Yeah, well I don't see why I should have it hotter than it was for anybody else.

BROADERS. It's no hotter than it ever was.

HUMPY. It is Broaders!

BROADERS. Zak, is that any hotter than it was for you or me?

ZAK. No, it's the very same.

HUMPY. It's not Zak.

BROADERS. Come on, will yeh, before it goes cold on me.

HUMPY. This better not hurt me, Broaders.

BROADERS. Hold his arm steady there, Zak. The mark of the Crab, Hah! Come on . . .

BROADERS *brings the knife blade down on* HUMPY*'s arm.* HUMPY *cries out in pain. Lights down.*

*

Lights rise on the kitchen where VERONICA *is busy, preparing the breakfast.*

VERONICA (*calling off*). Isaac, come on will yeh, your breakfast is ready.

ISAAC (*off*). What?

VERONICA. Come on, I'm puttin' your breakfast on the table now.

ISAAC (*off*). Right.

VERONICA *takes up the porridge and lays it on the table, etc.*

ISAAC (*entering*). Any sign of me Da yet?

VERONICA. No.

ISAAC. He's late, aint he? He must be gone out to the island to finish off me hut or somethin'

VERONICA. Sit down, will yeh.

ISAAC. Are you goin' down town today, Ma?

VERONICA. Probably, why?

ISAAC. Would yeh be able to get me a diary?

VERONICA. What are yeh wantin' a diary for?

ISAAC. I'm wantin' to write down everything that happens to me tomorrow night, like yeh know – goin' out to the island and all. Will you be able to get me one, though?

VERONICA. I don't know. We'll see. (*A sound overhead.*)

ISAAC. That sounds like one of me pigeons back already.

VERONICA. Stay where yeh are, you. Your pigeons will be alright.

ISAAC *whistles out to the pigeon.* SONIA *enters.*

SONIA. How are yeh, Veronica? Is Eagle here?

VERONICA. No. He went out fishin' last night Sonia and he's not back yet. Why? What are yeh wantin' him for?

SONIA. Ah, it's just that today's the last day if he's wantin' , to put his name down for that auld job that's goin' in the factory. Will he be long more, would yeh say?

VERONICA. I don't know to tell yeh the truth. He's never this late.

ISAAC. I'm tellin' yeh Ma he's gone out to finish off me hut. He's takin' me out to the island tomorrow night yeh know, Sonia.

SONIA. Yeah I know.

ISAAC. Anyway, there's no way is me Da goin' to go to work in that auld factory, Ma, and you know that. No way, boy!

SONIA. Shut up, you and eat your breakfast . . . What will I do, Veronica? Will I stick his name down anyway? I will. Sure, what harm, if he takes it, he takes it.

ISAAC. I'm tellin' yeh, Sonia, he won't work there.

SONIA. Ain't that awful, Veronica. (*She pretends to choke him.*)

ISAAC. How did yeh get on with your man after?

SONIA. Mind your own business, you.

VERONICA. Oh, that's right, you had a date with young Taylor last night, didn't yeh. Where did yeh go?

VERONICA *sorts through* ISAAC's *school bag and finds a catapult, which she takes and hangs by the door.*

SONIA. The Railway Hotel. We had a meal.

VERONICA. Is he nice?

SONIA. Yeah, he's alright. A bit grand, I suppose, but I'll tell yeh all about it tomorrow. The walls have ears here like, yeh know?

VERONICA. I know.

ISAAC. You should have heard what me Da said about him.

SONIA. What?

ISAAC. He said he wouldn't be runnin' that factory at all only he inherited it off his grandda.

SONIA. He'd hang yeh, wouldn't he?

ISAAC. Yeh should have seen him though, Ma. All the jewelry on him, boy! Great big rings on him and all. I'm not coddin' yeh, he was like King Farouk gettin' out of the car.

SONIA (*laughs*). He was too. But sure, it's good to see someone in the family goin' out with a bit of class ain't it?

VERONICA. Are yeh goin' to see him again?

SONIA. I don't know. I might. If I'm asked of course.

VERONICA. So, poor Zak is gone out of the picture altogether, now then yeah?

SONIA. Long ago. Where have you been girl? He turned up stocious drunk to see me one night and he had Broaders and that other latchico Humpy O'Brien hangin' out of him. I ran 'em. You're too soft with Eagle Veronica. Yeh should have put your foot down long and ever ago with him here. How long more is he goin' to hold out anyway. I mean he's not catchin' anythin' worth talkin' about lately, as far as I can see.

VERONICA. Yeah, well, yeh know Eagle. To tell yeh the truth, Sonia, I don't like to think of him workin' in that auld factory anyway . . . clockin' in and out of there and answerin' to someone and all.

SONIA. It's a pity about 'im.

VERONICA *sighs*.

VERONICA. No . . . he loves that auld boat though, yeh know. And he works hard.

SONIA. I know he works hard, Veronica, no one's sayin' he don't work hard. But it's not bringin' home the bacon though, is it? Well I'm goin' to stick his name down anyway. Listen I've to go. I'll drop in to see him this evenin'. You'll be after talkin' a bit of sense into him by then won't yeh?

VERONICA. Me! You must be jokin'. He's your brother, you can talk to him.

SONIA *leaves.* VERONICA *sighs.*

ISAAC. You're worse Ma. Sure you know as well as I do that me Da won't take a job there. No way, boy!

VERONICA. Yeah well, let's just hope he caught somethin' decent last night then.

ISAAC. Why?

VERONICA. Oh, no reason. Are you wantin' another sup of tea in that?

ISAAC. Yeah.

VERONICA. Yes, please!

ISAAC. Yes, please. Whist, there's another one of me pigeons back I'd say.

VERONICA. Finish your breakfast, will yeh.

ISAAC *whistles out to the pigeons.* EAGLE *enters, a salmon in each hand.*

ISAAC. How did yeh get on Da?

EAGLE *holds the fish aloft.*

Alright! There's a couple of me pigeons back already, Da.

EAGLE (*laying the fish down in a box by the door*). So I see.

ISAAC. They got back before yeh Da, hah?

EAGLE. Yeah.

ISAAC. Where did yeh let them off?

EAGLE. Useless Island.

ISAAC. Not too bad for their first time out though, Da, is it? They'll come home all the time now, won't they?

EAGLE. Oh, yeah.

VERONICA. Sonia was here lookin' for yeh. Did yeh see her?

EAGLE. I saw her goin' down the bank there. I wasn't talkin' to her or anythin'. What did she want?

VERONICA. She said today's the last day if you're wantin' to put your name down for that job that's goin' in the factory.

EAGLE *thinks about it. He shrugs.*

EAGLE. What do yeh think?

VERONICA. It's up to you.

EAGLE. Of the fish, I mean.

VERONICA *sighs and turns away.*

ISAAC (*crossing to examine the fish*). Don't mind them, Da, the pair of them are only tryin' to sell yeh down the river here boy.

VERONICA. Isaac, you get back to the table and finish your breakfast and stop actin' the auld man all the time.

ISAAC. I'm finished. These are two right ones alright, Da, ain't they? They should fetch a few bob alright, shouldn't they? Hah?

EAGLE (*at the sink*). Yeah.

ISAAC. Will I bring them over to the factory for yeh Da before I go to school?

EAGLE. If yeh like.

ISAAC. Auld Mosey'll get some land when he sees these won't he? He was sayin' only the other day that there's hardly anythin' worth catchin' out there anymore.

EAGLE. Yeh have to know where to look for them yeh see.

ISAAC. Oon the Da boy?

EAGLE. Hah?

ISAAC. Did yeh do any more work on the hut?

EAGLE. Yeah. Tomorrow night's the night boy! Hail, rain or snow.

ISAAC. Does the hut look alright though?

EAGLE. Yeah, it looks grand to me anyway.

ISAAC. Is it big?

EAGLE. Big enough.

ISAAC. Is it the same as the one you had when you were a young fella?

EAGLE (*taking off his boots*). More or less. The only difference is you have a bed raised up off the ground. I had to sleep on the floor – a rake of stones stickin' in me back all night long. Yeh might get us me slippers up under the bed there, Isaac, will ya?

ISAAC. What? Yeah right. I can't wait to see it boy. The smell of your feet, Da!

ISAAC *leaves. Pause.*

VERONICA. You're not serious about this, are yeh?

EAGLE. How do you mean?

VERONICA. You're wantin' to leave the child alone on a pitch black island in the middle of winter.

EAGLE. But sure, it's only a stone's throw away woman. I mean what's goin' to happen to him anyway? Nothin's goin' to happen to him.

VERONICA. He could fall into the fire. He could fall into the water. His hut could go up in a blaze or some queer fella might happen on him. I mean to say . . . anythin' could happen to him. And he's not well either, his chest is still at him.

EAGLE. Go away, it'll harden him up a bit.

VERONICA. He's hard enough.

EAGLE. He's too soft, Veronica. He needs to harden up a bit or they'll walk on him.

VERONICA. Too soft me eye, did you know that he was fightin' again out on the street yesterday. I had to go out after him. Too soft is right. Jaysus yeh won't be happy until yeh have him as bad as yourself – pigeons and dogs and boats!

She goes outside to fetch milk. ISAAC *returns.*

ISAAC. There's two more of me pigeons back now, Da.

EAGLE. Did yeh put them in?

ISAAC. Yeah I went out on the roof an put 'em in.

EAGLE. Good. Hey what's all of this I hear about you fightin' out in the street yesterday, eh?

ISAAC. Who told yeh that?

EAGLE. Your Mammy's just after tellin' me there. What were you fightin' for?

ISAAC. I don't know. He said somethin' about me Aunty Sonia.

EAGLE. What did he say about her?

ISAAC. I don't know. I don't remember.

EAGLE. Did yeh win?

ISAAC. It was a draw.

EAGLE. Yeh lost then.

ISAAC. I didn't lose Da. It was a draw I said.

EAGLE. Isaac, how many times do I have to tell yeh? There's no such thing as a draw in a fight, yeh either win or yeh lose. Now which was it?

ISAAC. I won, of course, only for me Ma came out and stopped I would have killed him.

VERONICA. Isaac, were you out on that roof?

ISAAC. Yeah, I went out to put me pigeons in.

VERONICA. Well I hope yeh closed that window after yeh, did yeh? I don't want them cats gettin' in again.

ISAAC (*putting on his jacket*). Yeah I closed it. I'll bring the fish over to the factory for yeh now, Da.

EAGLE. Yeah, right. Make sure yeh get a docket for them. And tell auld Mosey I'll be over to get me money meself as soon as I get a bit of sleep.

ISAAC. Alright.

VERONICA. You don't stay too long over there Isaac or you'll be late for school, do yeh hear me?

ISAAC. Yeah. But sure, he never says anythin' to me now anyway. I'm the teacher's pet since you joined the school committee. Did yeh know that Da? (*He retrieves the catapult.*)

EAGLE. What?

ISAAC. Mister Collins, the teacher, is mad about me Ma.

EAGLE. What?

VERONICA. Don't mind him. Go ahead. And listen, be careful goin' down that auld bank.

EAGLE. Yeah, mind my fish.

ISAAC *leaves.* VERONICA *throws* EAGLE *a dirty look. Lights down.*

*

Lights rise. It is early morning. We are outside the factory gates. BRIDIE *is having a quick smoke.* SONIA *enters, late for work.* ZAK *and* BROADERS *are sitting on top of a stack of mussel sacks.* HUMPY *is steeping his arm in the water barrel.* DRIBBLER *enters.*

DRIBBLER. Whenever you fellas are ready now. What's supposed to be wrong with him, eh! (*Referring to* HUMPY.)

ZAK. I don't know, Dribbler. A big crab is after bitin' him on the arm, I think.

HUMPY. Very funny, Zak.

DRIBBLER. Give us that auld song now, Bridie.

BRIDIE. You'll be lucky . . . What ails him? (*Humpy.*)

BROADERS. Who, Zak? He's broken hearted, Bridie. Sonia is after givin' him the big heave-ho sure. Did yeh know that, Dribbler?

DRIBBLER. What?

BROADERS. Sonia.

DRIBBLER. What about her?

BROADERS. She's after givin' Zak the shove in order to go out with a little nancy boy in an office.

DRIBBLER. Aye?

BROADERS. What do yeh think of that, Bridie?

BRIDIE. But sure a change is as good as a rest, Dribbler, ain't it?

DRIBBLER. Now yeh said it, Bridie.

BROADERS. Well, that was always your motto anyway, Bridie, wasn't it, Hah? (*He sings.*) . . . I let my hair down. I slipped my drawers off. Danced like an angel but I still didn't win his heart . . .

BRIDIE. I think I'd be wastin' me time droppin' me drawers in front of you, somehow or other.

HUMPY *laughs.*

BROADERS. I don't know, Bridie!

BRIDIE. He's like a jackdaw when he laughs, ain't he? Stick a feather up his hole now and he'd nearly fly away.

BRIDIE *exits. The boys laugh.*

BROADERS. What do yeh think of that, Zak? Sonia walkin' to work, be Jaysus! You'd think your man'd give her a lift in the mornin's, at least, wouldn't yeh? Hah?

ZAK. Will you go and cop on to yourself, Broaders.

BROADERS *laughs.* MOSEY *enters.*

MOSEY. I hope you fellas are comfortable there now, are yez?

BROADERS. Yeah.

MOSEY. Where are these out of now? (*The mussel sacks.*)

DRIBBLER. Just behind the shelter there.

MOSEY. And is that the last of them?

DRIBBLER. No, I'd say we'll get another load out of her.

MOSEY. Right. Well I suppose yeh'd better start gettin' them in to them.

DRIBBLER. Right lads, come on. Start shiftin' them.

BROADERS. Here you two, come on, Meself and Dribbler'll take in the next one.

HUMPY *goes around to the back of the trolley and starts pushing.* ZAK *goes to the front.*

MOSEY. What's there anyway? Three dozen?

DRIBBLER. Forty bags.

BROADERS. Look at him, he's a weak. (*Humpy.*)

DRIBBLER. Bring back some empty sacks and yeh comin' Zak, will ye?

BROADERS. Yeah and yeh needn't bother stayin' in there half the day either, chattin' up that young one!

MOSEY. He'd better not.

BROADERS. Zak is ragin'. What are yeh blushin' for Zak?

ZAK *gives* BROADERS *the V sign.* BROADERS *chuckles.* ZAK *and* HUMPY *exit.*

Strange auld world we're livin' in too though lads, ain't it? Hah? Your man there wants a girl that he can't have and this fella here is after a woman that nobody else wants. I don't know.

DRIBBLER. What can yeh do with a fella like that Mosey, eh?

MOSEY. Don't ask me.

DRIBBLER. See that – even your grandda don't understand yeh.

BROADERS. That's what I say – I'm misunderstood!

BRIAN *emerges over the crumbling wall with a wooden chest. He is wearing a frogsuit, etc.*

BRIAN. Hey Dribbler, give us a hand here will yeh.

DRIBBLER. What? Yeah right . . . No rest for the wicked,
  boy . . . What have yeh got there Boss? Treasure Island, be
  Jaysus?

DRIBBLER carries the chest and lays it down.

MOSEY. Where did yeh find that, Boss?

BRIAN. Just below the shelter wall there. Open her up there,
  Dribbler.

DRIBBLER. Yeah, right. Put your hand to that, Mosey, will
  yeh. That's it. It's not too bad inside either lads, look.

MOSEY. Oh, that's a well made little casket, boy.

BRIAN. It is, ain't it?

*The chest is full of ropes and maps and books and other
mouldy stuff.*

DRIBBLER (*plucking a telescope from the chest*). Wait 'til I
  see what me Ma is up to.

MOSEY (*softly*). Marian!

BRIAN. Huh?

MOSEY *finds a beautiful, rough hewed bronze medallion
on a cord. It has an image of a beautiful woman etched into
it. He takes it from the chest and studies it with sad eyes as
he rolls it around in his hand.*

BRIAN. This auld chest used to belong to me grandfather one
  time Mosey. Look, there's his name there. Edward Taylor.
  You'd never know what you'd find in this would yeh?

MOSEY. No.

DRIBBLER. You'd want to be careful Boss. Yeh could find an
  auld will in there disinheritin' yeh or somethin'.

BRIAN. What? He must have threw it out the window in a fit
  of rage one day or somethin' Mosey hah?

MOSEY. That'd be him alright!

DRIBBLER. I can't see a thing through that.

BRIAN. What's that Mosey. (*He reads the inscription on the front of the medallion.*) Quia Multum Amavit Hah! . . . Hang on to that if yeh want Mosey. Yeh know I was just thinkin' that if we cleared out the bed of the shelter it'd be an ideal place for us to plant mussels wouldn't it?

MOSEY. But sure that's where most of the boys moor their little boats all the time.

BRIAN. I'm sure we could accommodate them somewhere else Mosey, I mean to say that'd be ideal for us wouldn't it?

MOSEY. It'd be handy alright.

BRIAN. We'll see Mosey, hah! Give us a hand with this yoke Dribbler, will yeh? (*The chest.*)

DRIBBLER. Yeah. Anythin' for a chocolate biscuit.

DRIBBLER *and* BRIAN *exit with the chest.*

BROADERS. He's only in the place a wet day, be Jaysus, and already he's tryin' to tell us where to moor our boats. He'll be lucky!

MOSEY. What's the matter with you? Did somebody do somethin' on yeh or somethin'?

BROADERS. What? (*He backs away from* MOSEY'*s honest eyes.*)

ISAAC (*entering with the salmon*). Here y'are Mosey? Me Da sent these over to yeh.

BROADERS. Bardógs be Jaysus? (*He steals the boy's catapult.*)

ISAAC. You shut up, Broaders. They're bigger than anythin' you ever caught anyway.

BROADERS. Yes a couple of sardines.

ISAAC. What do yeh think of them Mosey? Right ones ain't they? Yeh have to know where to look for them yeh see Mosey . . . He said that you're to give me a docket and he'll be over to collect the money himself later on – as soon as he gets a bit of sleep.

MOSEY. Right.

ISAAC. Should be worth a few bob Mosey hah?

MOSEY. Could be.

BROADERS. He'll be able to buy yeh a decent bike now so.

ISAAC. I have a bike Broaders.

BROADERS. Yeah, an auld crock of a yoke. Yeh can hear the rattle of it a mile and a half away.

ISAAC. But sure you've n'er a bike at all.

BROADERS. I tell yeh I'd sooner walk than to have to ride that thing that you have because the whole place do be laughin' at yeh. How much did he pay for it anyway – nothin'?

ISAAC. If he did then it's twice more than you paid for yours.

ZAK *and* HUMPY *enter.*

ZAK (*laughing*). Hey Broaders, Humpy is after gettin' the greatest slap in the gob he ever got.

BROADERS. What? Why?

ZAK. One of the boys inside put his hand up Bridie's skirt and she blamed Humpy. Look at the big red mark on his face.

HUMPY. No though, Zak, someone inside there is blackguardin' me and I'm goin' to tell yeh one thing but if I find out who it is they'll be gettin' a solicitor's letter in the post from me next week so they will.

BROADERS. Hey Dribbler, this fella is after molestin' your beloved in there, yeh know.

DRIBBLER (*entering*) . What?

BROADERS. He put his hand up her skirt.

DRIBBLER. Hey boy.

HUMPY. You shut up Broaders. Don't mind him Dribbler.

ZAK. She gave him the greatest slap in the gob that he ever got Dribbler. I'm not coddin' yeh.

They laugh.

DRIBBLER. I'm goin' to tell yeh one thing Mosey but your
   man is over the moon about all the things he's after findin'
   over the past few days here yeh know. I mean to say that
   auld chest is full of treasure and he has a cardboard box in
   there too that's full of stuff – books and files and photographs and ledgers and all the rest of it – a load of stuff
   belongin' to his auld grandda.

MOSEY. Aye?

DRIBBLER. Yeah. Well I'm after gettin' a right cowboy book
   out of it anyway, 'Duel in the Sun' by Chris Mortimer.
   You'll see me now about twelve o'clock tonight and I'll be
   walkin' bandy and everythin' after readin' this . . . Oon
   Isaac me boy! The size of the fish!

ISAAC. Me Da caught these last night Dribbler. What do yeh
   think of them?

DRIBBLER. Show, give us a look at them.

ISAAC. Right ones Dribbler, ain't they?

BROADERS. A couple of bardógs, be Jaysus.

HUMPY. Yeah, sardines on toast.

DRIBBLER. Deadly boy!

ISAAC. Did yeh know that me Da is takin' me out to the
   island tomorrow night Dribbler?

DRIBBLER. Yeah I know. Did he finish off your hut yet?

ISAAC. Not yet. He's goin' out to put the roof on it tonight he
   said and that'll be that then. He's after buildin' me a sort of
   a bed in it too, I think – raised up off the ground. That's no
   harm Mosey, is it?

MOSEY. Harm? No. Why?

ISAAC. No reason.

DRIBBLER. Jaysus they were the days though Mosey weren't
   they? Hah. Twelve years of age boy and yeh'd be sent out to
   spend the night alone on that auld island. You'd come back
   in the mornin' and you'd be afraid of nothin' or no one

again. There's three fellas there and they're afraid of their
lives to walk home alone in the dark at night after a dance.

HUMPY. Me Da was tellin' me somethin' about that alright
Dribbler. They used to set the hut on fire in the mornin' or
somethin' didn't they?

DRIBBLER. I'll never forget the mornin' I was comin' back. I
could feel the heat of the fire on the small of me back as I
was gettin' into the boat and I could hear the auld crackle of
the hut and that, yeh know. I was dyin' to turn around and
look back at it, boy I'm not coddin' yeh. You're not
supposed to look back at it yeh see. And as we were nearin'
the shore I could see all the people comin' out of their
houses and down the auld bank to the beach – women and
children and auld men and everythin' and they all wavin'
and callin' out to me and all. Jaysus it was really a magic
feelin' alright though. But sure your Da was the last boy to
do out to the island Isaac yeh know.

ISAAC *smiles.*

BROADERS. I don't think I'd fancy spendin' a night alone out
on an auld haunted island though lads would you? Hah?

ISAAC. Will you go away Broaders, it's not haunted.

BROADERS. It is. The Dempsey Twins – every Saturday
night!

ISAAC. Ha ha ha, Broaders, I'm goin' out on a Friday night.

BROADERS. Or Friday night, I meant to say though.

ISAAC. Yeah, sure, Broaders.

HUMPY. But sure there's an auld wild boar out there too this
weather yeh know. I was out there last week and I saw all
this wild boar shit all over the place out there.

BROADERS. Oh that's right, I was readin' somethin' about
that in the paper alright.

ISAAC. There's no such thing as wild boars in this country any
more, Broaders.

BROADERS. Yeah, and then yeh woke up.

ZAK. Leave him alone, Broaders, will yeh.

BROADERS. What?

ZAK. Leave the chap alone out of that.

BROADERS. Is there somethin' wrong with you or somethin'
Zak? Hah.

Slight pause.

BROADERS. I think yez are all gone soft in the head or
somethin'. Buildin' huts and settin' fire to them! That all
died out years ago! There's what yeh want now. The mark
of the crab burnt into your arm!

HUMPY. Yes!

BROADERS. Show them yours, Zak. Come on out of that will
yeh?

BROADERS *forces* ZAK *to roll up his sleeve. He holds
both their arms aloft.* HUMPY *joins them.*

Blood brothers, boy! Gullagullagoo!

DRIBBLER. There y'are now Mosey, that's what I've got to
put up with all day.

MOSEY. Come on Isaac, let's go. And we'll let these fellas get
back to work.

MOSEY *and* ISAAC *exit.*

DRIBBLER. Poor auld Eagle, hah! Yeh have to hand it to him
boy, he won't lie down.

BROADERS. What's it all in aid of though, Dribbler, that's
what I'd like to know. What's it all in aid of . . . ? Bardogs!

HUMPY. Sardines on toast!

DRIBBLER. Come on, before Mosey rears up on us all.

DRIBBLER *wheels around and gives* HUMPY *a playful
slap in the face.*

HUMPY. Hey Dribbler cut it out will yeh.

DRIBBLER. You keep your hands to yourself in future boy.

ZAK. You'd want to be careful Dribbler or you'll be gettin' a solicitor's letter in the post next week.

HUMPY. Very funny Zak. Give us a verse of *'You Need Hands'* now while you're at it.

The men laugh and go about their work. Lights down.

*

Lights rise. It is mid-morning. BRIAN *is out at the gate checking the clocking-in cards.* MOSEY *is sitting close by smoking his pipe. Across the way, behind the factory gates, we can see* BROADERS, ZAK, DRIBBLER *and* HUMPY *working, lugging the wet mussel sacks and loading them onto the trolley.* MOSEY *is looking at the medallion,* BRIAN, *entering, wonders about him.*

BRIAN (*takes a diary from his pocket*). I found this auld diary belongin' to me grandda inside there, Mosey.

MOSEY. Aye?

BRIAN. Yeah. I was readin' the first few pages of it. It seems he was delighted with himself when he discovered this place here. 'An abundance of seafood', says he, 'lies untapped just below the surface. I do believe I've found what I've been looking for. I'm hopin' it'll trace his rise to prominence in the area. But sure maybe I'll learn somethin' out of it Mosey, hah! Maybe it'll teach me how to handle all the boys if nothin' else. Because to tell yeh the truth there are times when I can't make head nor tail of them all. I mean to say one minute they're all over yeh and the next they'll turn around and nearly ate yeh, I don't know.

MOSEY. They've a strange way of showin' their affection alright haven't they?

BRIAN. They surely have. What did they all make of my grandda when he first arrived here, Mosey?

MOSEY. They didn't like him. He was too much of a what-do-you-call-it . . . a dictator! But sure most of them refused to work for him at first. Mind you things were a little better around here then than they are now. Your grandda didn't give a toss about any of them of course. He wasn't after their fish anyway. He wanted the crabs and the eels and the cockles and the mussels and all the other little auld slippery things that the rest of us thought we were kind of above catching. It was all out there to be taken – for nothin'. And boy was he the fella to take it too . . . It wasn't long until he prospered out of it. He built himself a mansion, drove around the place in a big Mercedes. Women and children is all he had workin' for him at first but soon some of the boys started bringin' him odds and ends – a bucket full of this, a box full of that. There was none of them mad about doin' it of course but most of them had no choice in the matter because they weren't catchin' anythin' worth talkin' about. He let it all go to rack and ruin then in the end, be Jaysus!

BRIAN. Someone told me that you never sold him anything, Mosey.

MOSEY. No.

BRIAN. How come?

MOSEY. Ah I don't know . . . But sure we're queer auld hawks up here like, yeh know.

BRIAN. Tell me about it. Any advice?

MOSEY (*rising*). Yeah – never point at the stars and don't go fishin' on Martin's Eve.

MOSEY *heads towards the gates.* BRIAN *watches him go, slightly perplexed.*

BRIAN. Nice one, Mosey. Hey, yeh might tell Broaders, I'm wantin' a word with him when you're in there, will yeh.

MOSEY. Yeah, right.

SONIA *arrives.*

SONIA. I'm wantin' to put me brother's name down for that auld job that's goin' here.

BRIAN. Who? Eagle? But I didn't think he wanted to work here.

SONIA. He's changed his mind.

BRIAN. Alright. Anything else?

SONIA. How do yeh mean?

BRIAN. Well I just thought when you're here yeh might want to ask me out again or somethin' . That's all.

SONIA. What? Who do you think yeh are eh, God's gift or somethin', Jesus!

BRIAN. What?

SONIA. Look, what happened between you and me last night as far as I'm concerned was . . . (*Words fail her.*)

BRIAN. I'm only jokin' yeh . . . Are yeh wantin' to come out for a drink with me tonight or what?

SONIA. I don't know. I might.

BRIAN. Yeah, well as soon as yeh make up your mind about it yeh might give us a shout will yeh.

Pause. SONIA *looks into his eyes.* BRIAN *smiles.* SONIA *chuckles.*

BRIAN. Will I pick yeh up at the house?

SONIA. OK.

BRIAN. About half seven?

SONIA. Twenty to eight. Pick me up at Eagle's place, though, will yeh? I'm wantin' to see him about somethin'.

BRIAN. Right.

BROADERS *arrives.*

BROADERS. Are you wantin' me?

BRIAN. Yeah, just a minute . . . I'll see yeh tonight Sonia.

SONIA. Yeah, right.

She looks into BROADERS' *angry eyes and leaves.*

BRIAN. It's about your time keepin', Broaders.

BROADERS. What about it?

BRIAN. I see you were late again two mornin's last week.

BROADERS. I wasn't late this mornin'.

BRIAN. No yeh weren't this mornin', but you were late yesterday mornin' and the mornin' before that too. And I see yeh never came back after dinner last Thursday at all.

BROADERS. Look, if you've a complaint about my work, just say so, will yeh and be done with it.

BRIAN. I've no complaints about your work.

BROADERS. No, I wouldn't think so either. Because I lift more than my fair share. I lift twice as much as any of them in a day – more than Dribbler or Zak or any of them.

BRIAN. Yeah, when you're here yeh do.

BROADERS. Well, I don't know what you're worryin' about last Thursday afternoon for anyway because there was nothin' to be done here. I saved yeh half a day's wages.

BRIAN. I would've found yeh somethin' to do, don't you worry about that.

BROADERS. Like what?

BRIAN. Cleanin' up the place inside, sweepin' the factory floor, whatever.

BROADERS. I'm employed to work on the trawler, not to sweep floors.

BRIAN. Look, Broaders, if you don't like the way I'm runnin' things around here, then there's plenty of other fellas that'll gladly take your place.

BROADERS. Are yeh done?

BRIAN. Yeah.

BROADERS. Right.

The siren blows. BRIAN *exits.* BROADERS *watches him go.* ZAK, HUMPY, BROADERS *and* DRIBBLER *are working out in front of the gates now.*

ZAK. What did he say to yeh, Broaders?

BROADERS. He's wantin' to give me a rise.

HUMPY. Yeah, up the arse, out the door.

BROADERS. Humpy, how would you like to find yourself standin' on your head in that auld water barrel for the next twenty minutes, eh?

All the men go to their coats for their sandwiches and flasks, etc. Some of the workers have gone out of the factory to sit in the open air. BRIDIE *comes across to join* DRIBBLER. SONIA *is sitting on the wall, away from the others.* ZAK *goes to her.*

HUMPY. Look at the size of that big crab Broaders crawlin' out of the dirty water. The size of the big claws of it! He's a mean old sonofabitch.

HUMPY *examines the crab mark on his arm.*

ZAK. Can I talk to yeh for a minute Sonia?

SONIA. What about?

ZAK. What do yeh think?

SONIA. Tch . . . there's no point, Zak. I mean forget it!

ZAK. Why though, Sonia, that's all I'm wantin' to know. Why?

SONIA. Why? Yeh two timed on me every chance yeh got, Zak, and you were turnin' up drunk all the time. And late. And the way yeh talk to me.

ZAK. What do yeh mean?

SONIA. Yeh talk to me as if I was one of the boys or somethin'. I'm not one of the boys, Zak. I'm a girl, a woman. Talk to Broaders like that if yeh want, but not to me.

ZAK. What do yeh mean, the way I talk to yeh like?

SONIA. Cursin' all the time and all. And puckin' me in the shoulder all the time. Yeh don't know how to treat a girl, Zak. Yeh haven't a clue how to treat a girl. Anyway I'm goin' out with Brian now so . . . What's so funny: Do yeh think that I'm not good enough for him or somethin'?

ZAK. I never said that.

SONIA. Well, what then?

ZAK. He's just not your type, that's all.

SONIA. What do yeh mean?

ZAK. For God's sake Sonia, he's a little nancy boy in an office.

SONIA. Yeah and I'm just a scrubber in a factory, is that it?

ZAK. He's a nancy boy in an office. I'd bate him with me hand tied behind me back. Do yeh think I wouldn"t? Get him out here then. Go ahead.

SONIA. Goodbye, Zak.

ZAK. Get him out here.

SONIA. I'd like to eat my lunch in peace, if yeh don't mind.

ZAK. What? Yeah, right.

He storms off back to the boys.

HUMPY. Yes, he's a mean old mother. A mean old mother of mine.

BROADERS *looks into* ZAK'*s eyes.* ZAK *shakes his head.*

BROADERS. That one's gettin' too high and mighty for herself if yeh ask me . . . (*Shouts.*) Like her brother!

SONIA *leaves in a huff.*

HUMPY. If you're too brokenhearted to eat all your sandwiches, Zak, I'll give yeh a hand if yeh like.

ZAK *throws him a dirty look. Pause.* DRIBBLER *and* BRIDIE *share their sandwiches.*

DRIBBLER. All the times we used to come here to pick the fruit when we were young, Bridie, hah? You used to have more strawberries on your face now than yeh ever put in your basket, and I used to have to top up your can for yeh all the time, so you'd make enough money to go to the pictures. Jaysus, this was a beautiful place then though, lads. Menapia Mansion! I know you'd never think to look at it now, but, it was . . . auld Taylor built it in his heyday. And all these gardens were all landscaped and all. It was really beautiful alright though Bridie, wasn't it?

BRIDIE. Yeah. It was. All the roses growin' down by the river. And the lilac on the orchard wall. Pear trees and peaches and plums and apples. And tomatoes growin' in the greenhouse. And the beautiful gardens! God, it did your heart good just to walk past here in the mornin's. And comin' home from a dance at night, all the boys and girls 'd always cut through here for a shortcut and it seemed to be summer all the time that time. The smell of the sea minglin' with the lonely auld smell of summer. This is where I learnt to pray to Mary Magdalen. Mosey's Marian taught me. God be good to her!

DRIBBLER. Mmm . . . Mary Meek and Mild, hah?

BRIDIE. Yeah. Mary Meek and Mary Mild. Mary Tame and Mary Wild. Mary Young and Mary Old. Mary Sad and Mary Bold.

BROADERS *takes out his catapult and fires at something in the distance.*

HUMPY. Nice one, Broaders.

BROADERS. Yup out of that.

HUMPY *runs offstage and begins trashing something to death with a stone, re-entering with the bloody carcass of a dead seagull.*

HUMPY. What will I do with it, Broaders?

BROADERS. Give it to Zak there.

HUMPY. What? Yeah, right. Here y'are Zak, put that between your bread boy.

HUMPY *throws the seagull at* ZAK *and laughs.* ZAK*, in a rage, picks up the dead bird and chases* HUMPY*offstage.* BROADERS *follows. Lights down.*

*

Lights rise on the yard. EAGLE, DRIBBLER *and* ISAAC *are present.* EAGLE *is making a catapult.*

DRIBBLER. Yeh know, what way you're fixed with a good cowboy book though lads, yeh know. Yeh know who's who and what's what and who's right and who's wrong and all the rest of it. I mean to say, it has everything – action, scenery, romance. Yeh know the prairies and the mountains and all that kind of stuff. Louis L'Amour, Eagle! A great writer boy! Did yeh ever read anythin' by him, no! Well I must have read nearly everything that fella ever wrote, 'River's West', 'A Man Called Noon', 'Heller With a Gun', 'Lando' . . . the whole shebang boy! Mastermind! The Life and Works of Louis L'Amour! There's one of the best cowboy books I ever read, though lads. 'Duel in the Sun'. It was written by a fella called Chris Mortimer. Accordin' to the blurb, he only wrote the one book and then he was killed tragically. Shot through the head by his jilted lover when she found him in the arms of another woman. She emptied a revolver into him. Classic stuff! It's a pity he didn't live to tell the tale says you, he could have had a bestseller on his hands.

ISAAC. What's it about, Dribbler?

DRIBBLER. Duel in the Sun? It tells the story of this auld agein' gunslinger who decided to hang up his guns and settle down in a little one-horse town, half the book shows yeh the auld fella goin' about his business in the small town while the other half tells yeh all about this young punk of a gunslinger, who's wantin' to make a name for himself, takin' on the auld lad . . . Well your man goes through hell and high water to get to the little town. Through the badlands of New Mexico, through Indian country and everything; drawn towards his destiny, as your man puts it. Meanwhile the auld lad is goin' about his business in the small town. Although he seems to sense trouble brewin' and everyday at noon . . .

Lights dim on the yard and rise on the kitchen where VERONICA *is at the mirror, applying her make-up as* EAGLE *enters from the yard.*

VERONICA. How much did yeh get for the salmon after?

EAGLE. Fifty-seven quid.

VERONICA. Where is it?

EAGLE. I have it here, well most of it like. I had to spend twenty-three quid on the wood for the hut.

VERONICA. But sure there's lashin's of auld wood out the back there that yeh could have used instead of . . .

EAGLE. I have used some of it. But I need special timber for the hut yeh see. 'Cause it all has to be tied together, yeh know. No nails nor nothin'?

VERONICA. Eagle, I had Sonia and young Taylor up with me this evenin' here and I hadn't a bloody biscuit in the house to give them and now you're tellin' me that you're after spendin' twenty-three pounds on wood for an auld hut that'll be burnt down tomorrow mornin'.

EAGLE. The hut has to be built in a certain way. It's a tradition.

VERONICA. Yeah well we have a tradition in this house too, Eagle. Like yeh know. When the rent is paid and there's plenty of food on the table, then we're entitled to play our little games.

EAGLE. What are yeh talking about – playin' games? Hah? What are yeh talkin' about?

VERONICA. You know well enough what I'm talkin' about Eagle. There's a job goin' over in that ould factory and you didn't even bother your arse goin' to see about it. I wouldn't mind but yeh promised me that if things didn't pick up soon you'd . . .

EAGLE. Things did pick up. I caught two salmon didn't I?

VERONICA. Yeah and yeh spent nearly half the money on an auld hut that'll be burned down tomorrow mornin'.

EAGLE. Lord Jaysus ain't that awful what I've to listen to too. I mean just because a man loves what he's doin', they're all down on him.

VERONICA. No one's down on yeh at all Eagle.

EAGLE. The hut has to be built in a certain way and that's all's about it.

VERONICA. Yeah, right.

VERONICA goes to the mirror again to apply her lipstick. EAGLE watches her transformation, jealously.

EAGLE. Where are yeh goin' anyway?

VERONICA. The Railway Hotel. School committee meetin'.

EAGLE. In the Railway Hotel! How come it's not in the school?

VERONICA. I don't know. The heatin's off or somethin'. I won't be late.

*

Lights rise on the yard where DRIBBLER *struts like a gunslinger as* ISAAC *listens wide-eyed to him.*

DRIBBLER. He just stood on the veranda in the shade and let the young fella come to him. The young lad walked up the deserted street, two guns on him, hangin' low down, a black hat on his head tied under his chin. He was in the shade too until he came to the mouth of this little alleyway and then the noonday sun came blastin' over the rooftops, blindin' him, and that's when the auld fella made his move. As soon as the young lad squinted the auld fella reached for his holster and gunned him down. Cute yeh see! Duel in the Sun.

DRIBBLER twirls an invisible gun nimbly on his finger and then he shoots his imaginary opponent with a gun in his other hand. He blows the smoke away and enters the kitchen as VERONICA *comes into the yard.*

VERONICA. Isaac, you look after the place 'til I come back – won't yeh?

ISAAC. Yeah, right. Dribbler's a right bit a laugh, Ma, ain't he?

VERONICA. Yeah, hilarious!

*

Lights rise. BRIDIE *is sitting on a trolley outside the factory gates.* ZAK, BROADERS *and* HUMPY *enter, crying out.*

HUMPY. Thumbelina Nolan boy.

ZAK. Knows her way around. Gullagullagoo!

BROADERS. Oon Bridie boy!

HUMPY. Hey Bridie, Dribbler is up in the pub lookin' for you, yeh know.

BRIDIE. Is he?

BROADERS. Don't mind him, Bridie. You stay where you are hon. That fella is only wantin' to throw a rake of drink into yeh so he can take advantage of yeh . . . Give us a kiss, I wants to be sick.

He leans on her.

BRIDIE. Get away from me, yeh little animal yeh.

BROADERS. Ah, I'm only jokin' yeh, Bridie, Bridie!

HUMPY. Yeh sang well tonight Bridie, fair play to yeh. (*He sings, almost monotone.*) I let my hair down, I slipped my shoes off, Danced like an angel . . .

BROADERS. You should learn to sing a different song Bridie. People don't like listenin' to someone singin' the same auld song all the time, yeh know.

HUMPY. We'll have to write one for her Broaders.

BROADERS. Yeah. (*He sings.*)
Oh, I am the village bicycle
And they come from miles around;
To ride me up and down this cosy little town;

Oh, hurry up, kind sir, hurry up kind sir says she,
Oh, the angelus is ringing and I must go home for tea . . .

HUMPY (*laughs and sings*).
I let my drawers down,
I slipped me knickers off . . .

BROADERS. Hey, Bridie, would yeh be able to fix Humpy here up with that new one that started in the factory the other day, there?

HUMPY. You shut up, Broaders.

BROADERS. What's her name? Anita?

HUMPY. Don't mind him Bridie.

BROADERS. Just tell her that if she agrees to go out with him, we'll all chip in and buy her a guide dog.

HUMPY. Very funny, Broaders.

BROADERS *laughs. He runs to the gates and begins shaking them, furiously.*

BROADERS. Let me in, let me in, I wants to go to work. I'm addicted to it. Let me in . . . Please!

HUMPY *looks at him and laughs.*

HUMPY. What age is she anyway, Bridie?

BRIDIE. Who?

HUMPY. Anita.

BRIDIE. She's old enough to have more sense than to go out with a gobshite like you.

HUMPY. What?

BRIDIE *throws him a dirty look.* HUMPY *backs away.*
BROADERS *sniggers and looks across at* ZAK, *sitting on top of a pile of mussel sacks, gazing wistfully into space.*

BROADERS. Oh, to be in love, hah! Were yeh ever in love, Bridie? No? . . . Neither was I. Not accordin' to that, anyway. (*Nodding towards* ZAK.) Oh! Speakin' of love!

SONIA *and* BRIAN *enter.*

BRIAN. Have you fellas no homes to go to?

HUMPY. How's it goin'?

BRIAN. How are yeh, Bridie?

BRIDIE. How are yeh.

BROADERS. Must have forgot his spectacles lads.

BRIAN (*opening the lock on the gates*). What's that?

BROADERS. I say did yeh forget somethin' , yeah?

BRIAN. Somethin' like that.

SONIA. I'll hang on here for yeh, Brian.

BRIAN. Right. I won't be a minute.

He exits.

BRIDIE. Where did yeh go?

SONIA. We went down to the Railway Hotel. We just had a
few drinks, that's all.

BROADERS. Did yeh sit at the bar or was it waiter service?
Hey Sonia, what's goin' on here, anyway? I hope this fella
is not knockin' off the factory on the sly now or anythin'
The culprit was apprehended comin' out of the factory gates
with a pocket full of mussels and a mouthful of lobster. He
had a big slippery eel down the front of his trousers and a
sack full of mussels stuffed up the back of his jumper.
When asked to identify himself, he answered to the name of
Humpy O'Brien.

HUMPY. Hey. Broaders, watch it.

BROADERS. To further disguise himself he had to whip off
one of his ears, cut out one of his eyes, spit out a handful of
teeth and grow a mangy auld beard down one side of his
face but even still the police sergeant could see that he was
far too good lookin' to be the man he claimed to be.

HUMPY. Very funny Broaders, tell me when to laugh.

BROADERS. Cut off his testicles someone said. No, no, his
girlfriend cried, they're mine, all mine.

SONIA. Do yeh know somethin' Broaders but you really should try washin' yourself sometime because there's an awful smell of fish off of yeh, yeh know.

BROADERS. And what do yeh think you smell of, eau de cologne or some fuckin' thing?

HUMPY. Broaders is ragin'. Yeh see, Broaders, it doesn't matter how smart yeh think yeh are, you'll still get your comeuppance sooner or later boy. Yeh could be the smartest lad in the world, but you'll always meet someone who's smarter than yeh.

BROADERS *shakes his head and sighs. He goes to* ZAK.

BROADERS. Yes, oh, to be in love!

ZAK. What?

BROADERS. Here he is now . . . (BRIAN *is returning.*) The walk of him! (*They laugh.*) Is everything alright in there, yeah?

BRIAN (*locking up*). Yeah.

BROADERS. That's good . . . you're not from around here, are yeh?

BRIAN. No.

BROADERS. I thought that . . . so how come yeh came to be so well up on the dirty little world of the slippery auld eel then? Did yeh go to college and read up on it or somethin', yeah?

BRIAN. That's right.

BROADERS. For how long?

BRIAN. Three years.

BROADERS. Three years! Jaysus, you should have come out with me. I could have taught yeh all yeh needed to know in a fortnight. Mind you, yeh need to have the stomach for it. The auld trawler is inclined to be a bit bumpy at times like, yeh know.

BRIAN. Oh, I think I'd've managed alright, Broaders, don't worry about that.

BROADERS. What? Oh that's right, sure you're a bit of a deep sea diver ain't yeh? I forgot all about that. Yeah! Jacques Cousteau the Second, hah! Not like you and me, Humpy, divin' off the shelter wall in the summer.

HUMPY. Yeah or walkin' the greasy pole during the regatta.

Pause.

BROADERS. So, what do yeh think of the place, anyway?

BRIAN. Grand. Great, really. Good people. Great stories to tell. Everywhere I go nearly I hear a different story – about the Dempsey twins and that. Dribbler was tellin' me that one this mornin' there.

BROADERS. Yeah, well, I wouldn't pay much attention to all of that, if I was you. Up around here, they'll only tell yeh what they think yeh want to hear.

BRIAN. Ah no, they were genuine stories, alright. I find all that stuff interestin' anyway, like yeh know.

HUMPY. By Jaysus and we could tell yeh some hairy stories, I don't mind tellin' yeh. Couldn't we, lads? Do yeh remember the night we went to the dance in Enniscorthy? (*He laughs.*)

BRIAN. Oh, I dare say, Humpy, the day'll come when your name'll be trippin' off the tips of the tongues of people who are not even born yet, boy!

BROADERS. I gravely doubt that somehow or other.

BRIAN. Ah well, yeh see people don't always realise that they're livin' interestin' lives, yeh know.

BROADERS *scoffs.*

SONIA. I think what Brian means is that . . .

BROADERS. I know what he means . . .

Silence.

BRIAN. See yeh in the mornin', lads.

HUMPY. Good luck.

BROADERS. All the breast . . .

They leave. BROADERS *calls after them.*

Try and get in on time in the mornin', if yeh can will yeh.

HUMPY. Come on and we'll follow them Broaders will we, see what they're up to. Come on. I'm goin' to follow them. Come on. Are yeh comin' Zak, come on . . .

HUMPY *exits.* BROADERS *goes to* BRIDIE. *He gazes up at the starry sky.*

BROADERS. There's no one out there yeh know Bridie.

BRIDIE. What?

BROADERS. There's no one out there. There's no one watchin' over us or anythin'. Nobody's keepin' tabs on all the things we do and say to one another. And do yeh know what that means Bridie? It means we can do what we want. We can say what we like. Because there's no one out there. Nobody gives a shit! Here, wait 'til I show yeh this. (*He takes out a knife.*) Do yeh see this? Do yeh see that big crab that's welded into the blade there? Well, he's sort of my hero, yeh know. Yeah, that fella crawls out of the muddy waters everyday of his workin' life and he sets off in a straight line devourin' everythin' he sees. He don't give no one nothin'. He just takes what he wants and leaves the rest behind him. And right, you may say to me that at any time any one of us could just step on him and crush him to death and that'd be that, but that's not the point. While he's alive, as long as he exists, he's the kingpin around here. He's the one who rules the roost. And that's the reason. That's why he's my hero. (*He takes the knife back.*) And he don't need to tell no stories either, Bridie, and he don't need to listen to them. And do yeh know somethin'? Neither do I . . . No, there's no one out there.

BROADERS *exits. Pause.*

ZAK. Would yeh be able to put a word in with Sonia for me Bridie?

BRIDIE. What?

ZAK. Would yeh be able to put a word in with her for me?

BRIDIE. How do yeh mean? I mean what do yeh want me to say to her?

ZAK. I don't know. Just put a word in for me like.

BRIDIE. Look, Zak, why don't yeh just let her go now. You're a good lookin' fella. You could have lashin's of girls after yeh. Let her go. Sonia has a chance of gettin' out of here now. So why not let her take it?

ZAK. What do yeh mean?

BRIDIE sighs. Looks into his eyes and runs her fingers gently through his hair.

BRIDIE. You are a good lookin' fella, yeh know. Yeh remind me of a boy I used to know one time. He was a bit wild, too and all mixed up on the inside just like you are now. But unfortunately, he was just about to get married to someone else, when it all began. For three solid weeks, I met him every night behind Menapia Mansion there – under the Rose! It was probably just a last wild fling as far as he was concerned, but I fell hook, line and sinker for him. I swear I've never met anyone like him before or since. And God knows I've looked . . . I never told anyone about it. I never let the cat out of the bag on him. I don't think he even realised I was in trouble to tell you the truth. Well, if he did he never acknowledged it, anyway, let's put it that way. It was a baby boy – we buried him in a little overgrown grave with a wooden cross to mark the spot. Me Da painted the child's name on it but the rain came that night and washed it away . . . If he had've lived he would have been thirteen tomorrow – the tenth of November, St Martin's Eve – and I'd be singin' a different song today than the one I'm singin' now. Let her go, Zak. I know it's hard but sometimes when yeh love someone yeh just have to let them go.

ZAK. I can't Bridie. Me heart is sort of set on her, yeh see. Yeh might put in a word for me if yeh get the chance, will yeh.

ZAK leaves. Lights down.

*

Lights rise. BRIAN *and* SONIA *are sitting together in the little graveyard.*

BRIAN (*reading from the diary*). Here it is. Listen to this. 'Saw her today for the very first time – a magnificent lookin' woman with a mane of coal black hair and a pair of fiery eyes. Like a magnet she drew me towards her. She had come to sell me a bucketful of the loveliest looking oysters I've ever seen. I asked her where she found them and she offered to show me the place tomorrow . . . I met her . . . ' No, I can't make it out. 'She led me across the rocks on the far side of Useless Island and just opposite the . . . ' What's that?

SONIA. The Black Man.

BRIAN. 'Just opposite the Black Man we . . . ' something, something . . . 'I was not thinking of oysters. My mind was elsewhere. She smelt of the sea. Everything about her – her hair, her face, her hands, her breath even. She was like a creature that had risen up out of the sea to come and live amongst us. I wanted to throw myself down at her feet, I wanted to live inside of her . . . ' I can't believe this. I mean, I remember me grandfather as a real cranky old man with hardly anything to say for himself. We used to come here as children for the summer holidays and I swear he never put any pass on us at all. He used to lock himself away in a dark room – poutin' lips and smellin' of whisky. We were all afraid of our lives of him, and here he is cavorting with a married woman.

SONIA. He sounds like a fairly passionate man then.

BRIAN. He does, doesn't he?

SONIA. I wonder who she is. Does it say who she is? (BRIAN *shakes his head.*) When was all this supposed to have happened anyway?

BRIAN. Oh, I don't know. Forty years ago nearly, now.

SONIA. Read some more.

BRIAN (*chuckles, kisses her and reads*). 'Today I plucked up the courage to venture to kiss her. She responded to me,

I took her in my arms.' This is incredible! . . . 'I took her in my arms . . . ' I can't make out the rest of that page. It's all smudged. Just as well I think. But wait 'til yeh hear this. 'Stole away last night to Useless Island for another night of bliss' – another night of it if yeh don't mind! And here's the best part. 'We had a close shave when her husband passed not four feet from where we lay. She shivered in my arms with the fright and I had to comfort her . . . ' Jesus!

SONIA. I wonder if they ever came up here.

BRIAN. They probably did. They probably sat right here where we're sittin' now. And then she laid back in the long grass.

SONIA. Here?

BRIAN. Yeah.

SONIA. Yeah?

Slight pause. BRIAN *rises and goes to her. He takes her in his arms, they kiss, slumping onto the ground. Suddenly she stops him, gazing off into the distance.*

BRIAN. What's up?

SONIA. Humpy O'Brien is watchin' us.

BRIAN. What? Where?

SONIA. Over there by the gate. Do yeh see him? Tch, he's an awful ejit, that fella is . . . Come on.

BRIAN. What?

SONIA *rises and straightens her attire.* BRIAN *does likewise. They leave.* HUMPY *enters, hiding behind the tree and running from grave to grave. He finds the diary that* BRIAN *has left behind. He pockets it as* BROADERS *enters.*

HUMPY. Ah, yeh missed it, Broaders, boy.

BROADERS. What?

HUMPY. She was lyin' down there with him and everythin', Broaders. Yeh missed it, boy!

BROADERS. How do yeh know?

HUMPY. Because I was watchin' them. The pair of them were
sittin' down here where they thought they couldn't be seen.
He got her down onto the ground then and she started atin'
the face off of him and everythin', boy. It bet the bun
altogether here, so it did. She's some bitch though, ain't
she? Hah? Zak'll go mad, boy. Right beside your granny's
grave, too, Broaders hah! No respect, boy! I'm goin' to tell
yeh one thing too, but I wouldn't say she's the first girl to
come up here with that fella either since he arrived, would
you? I'd say that lad's a real whoremaster altogether goin'
around, would you? Hah?

BROADERS. That's for sure. He's makin' whores out of the
whole lot of us here as far as I can see.

HUMPY. How do yeh mean?

BROADERS. But sure he has us all where he wants us now,
hasn't he? Clockin' in and out of that place for him every
day. Luggin' and draggin' and sweepin' floors and all the
rest of it. No matter where we're workin', yeh know, he can
see us out of his office window. It doesn't matter where we
are – out in the auld trawler or unloadin' on the shore or
down in the shelter. It makes no odds, he can see us. And
he's always watchin' too – always lookin' and checkin'.
We're just dirt under his fingernails, that's all we are to him.
Dirt, boy. We're no better than the auld crabs and eels that
we have to catch for him. Dirt!

HUMPY. That's a fact alright. Did yeh ever see the way he
looks at yeh. He has a real dirty eye, hasn't he? 'Your
name'll be trippin' off the lips of their tongues', says he!
The voice on him, we're just dirt under his fingernails, boy.
Yes, whores he's after makin' of the whole lot of us here,
ain't he? Hah?

BROADERS. Yeah. I'm afraid so.

HUMPY. The whoremaster anyway. (*Shouts.*)
WHOREMASTER!

HUMPY *hides down out of sight.* BROADERS *just stands
there.*

HUMPY. Get down, Broaders. Get down, will yeh. Broaders! He's watchin'. He's lookin'. He'll see yeh, Broaders!

BROADERS *staring off into the distance. Lights down.*

*

Lights rise on the kitchen. It is the following night. SONIA *is packing stuff into a cardboard box.* MOSEY *is sitting, smoking, a few boxes at his feet.* ISAAC *is writing in his diary.* VERONICA *arrives with another box containing all the stuff for* ISAAC'*s trip, blankets and sleeping bags, food and hot water bottles, etc.*

VERONICA. Where's Eagle?

MOSEY. He's just gone down to the boat for a minute. He said you were all to wait here for him.

VERONICA. Right. Have you got a packet of tea bags there, Sonia?

SONIA. Yeah, they're here, look.

VERONICA. Give them to me, will yeh. I'm wantin' to keep all the food stuff together if I can. Here, put those toilet rolls in your box Sonia. All the food stuff is in this little box here Isaac, look.

ISAAC. Right. (ISAAC *is writing in his diary.*)

VERONICA. Tell your Daddy that I put a few firelights in this brown bag here.

ISAAC (*writing*). Right.

VERONICA. Were my eyes deceivin' me or did I see Humpy O'Brien goin' by my window tonight with a girl?

SONIA. Yeah. The boys fixed him up with this new one that started in the factory.

VERONICA. God, she must have no one belongin' to her then to go out with him.

SONIA. Did yeh see the state of the suit on him. He's like somethin' the cat dragged in.

They laugh.

ISAAC. What date is this, Ma?

VERONICA. What? St Martin's eve – the tenth of November.

SONIA. What are yeh doin', Isaac?

ISAAC. I'm writin' it all into me diary.

SONIA. I never knew you kept a diary.

ISAAC. I only got it today sure.

VERONICA. Bridgey Malloy sent yeh over a cake too, Isaac. Look.

ISAAC. Yeah, I know.

VERONICA. Yeh should feel the weight of it, Sonia, it's like an anchor, so it is, I don't know what the hell she puts in it, at all.

ISAAC. Is this alright, Sonia? Today's the day that I go out to the island. I can't wait to see my little hut. Bridgey Malloy sent me over a cake and Mosey Brennan gave me a big medal of a beautiful woman. Me Aunty Sonia promised me a pound if I come back alive.

SONIA (*chuckles*). That's great, Isaac. You should write it all down now – whatever happens tonight.

ISAAC. That's what I'm goin' to do, sure.

SONIA. Yeah? What do you think, Mosey? Do yeh think Isaac should write it all down tonight?

MOSEY. Yeah. As long as he spells my name right, of course.

ISAAC. M.O.S.E.Y. Mosey!

SONIA (*examining the medallion around* ISAAC'*s neck*). Who is that, anyway, Mosey?

MOSEY. I don't know. The patron saint of the disappointed, apparently!

ISAAC. I hope I won't be, Mosey, hah!

MOSEY *nods sadly.*

SONIA (*reads the back of the medallion*)
  Mary meek and Mary mild
  Mary tame and Mary wild
  Mary young and Mary old
  Mary sad and . . .

  EAGLE *enters.*

EAGLE. Alright, lads? Is everythin' nearly ready, yeah?

VERONICA. Yeah.

ISAAC. I'm bringin' me diary out to the island with me Da.

EAGLE. Yeah? That's good. There's a good crowd down there
  mind yeh Mosey.

MOSEY. Aye?

EAGLE. Did yeh hear that, Isaac, there's a good crowd down
  there to see yeh off, boy. You've packed enough stuff for
  him anyway, Veronica. Anyone'd think he was goin' out for
  a month or somethin'.

VERONICA. Better to be sure than sorry. (*She is helping*
  ISAAC *into a big hooded anorak.*) Yeh stuck in those few
  extra blankets for him, Sonia, didn't yeh?

SONIA. Yeah.

EAGLE. He won't need all that stuff, Veronica. Sure, I'm after
  buildin' him a hut out there, man, and it's like a little igloo,
  so it is.

VERONICA. What do yeh think the child is, an Eskimo or
  somethin'?

ISAAC. I'm goin' to tell yeh one thing, but I feel like a feckin'
  Eskimo in this thing.

VERONICA. You stop that cursin' boy.

MOSEY. I threw an auld ground sheet into the end of the boat
  for yeh, Eagle. Keep out some of the damp.

EAGLE. Oh, thanks, Mosey. Although I'm after buildin' him a sort of a bed in it to raise him up off of the ground.

MOSEY. So I heard. Jaysus, it's a wonder you didn't put a lav and everythin' in it and yeh at it.

EAGLE. Modern times, Mosey . . . we may make two trips down to the boat, Isaac, I think.

VERONICA. Yeh won't need to make two trips at all. Meself and Sonia'll give yeh a hand.

EAGLE. Alright then, come on, let's go.

MOSEY. Are you rowing out or what?

EAGLE. No. Sail.

VERONICA. Now you remember what I was sayin' to yeh, Isaac, and stay well clear of that fire once your Daddy is gone. Do yeh hear me?

ISAAC. Yeah.

VERONICA. Eagle, you won't light that fire too close to the hut now, sure, yeh won't?

EAGLE. No.

VERONICA. And stay clear of the water's edge, too, hon' won't yeh? I've an awful fear of him fallin' into the water, Sonia.

SONIA. Oh, he'll be alright, Veronica.

ISAAC. With this big bloody thing on me, I'll probably float anyway. (*The women chuckle.*) If you're wantin' to kiss me now or anythin', Ma I'd advise yeh to do it now because there's no way you're doin' it down there in front of everyone.

VERONICA. Ain't that awful, Sonia?

VERONICA *puts her arms around him and hugs and kisses him.* SONIA *does likewise.* EAGLE *picks up a box and makes to leave.*

EAGLE. Whenever yez are ready now!

They leave, ISAAC *doubling back for his diary. Lights down.*

EAGLE (*calling out*). Come on Isaac!

*

Lights rise on the graveyard. BROADERS *is standing over a grave.* ZAK *is sitting beneath the tree, gazing out to sea.*

ZAK. Maybe we should have gone down to see him off, hah?

BROADERS. What for?

ZAK. Ah, I don't know. It feels kind of queer to find yourself on the outside lookin' in, don't it?

BROADERS. Not if that's where yeh want to be.

BROADERS *turns away.* ZAK *watches him.* VERONICA *enters.*

VERONICA. Any sign of them, Zak?

ZAK. Yeah, they're just goin' round by the Black Man now, there. Can yeh see them? They're nearly out there now sure . . . He had a fair auld send off after anyway didn't he?

VERONICA. Yeah. (*She looks at* BROADERS.) Sayin' a few prayers for his granny is he?

ZAK. Yeah.

VERONICA. Poor Marian. God all the times I went across to tell her me troubles. She was one great bit of stuff so she was. Sure poor Mosey is lost without her. And she was the only one who was ever able to get any good of that young lad . . . Mary Meek and Mild hah! Sometimes yeh have to wonder what it's all about Zak don't yeh? Yeh live and yeh die and then they put yeh down a big hole to rot. Sure no wonder people go to so much trouble to put their mark on the world while they're here.

She looks out to sea.

HUMPY (*entering*). I'm goin' to tell yeh one thing, Zak but
she's some snobby bitch boy . . . Hello Missus. Do yeh
know where she wanted to go Zak? The Railway Hotel!
Says I to her, 'If the Shark public house is not good enough
for you then you can say goodbye to me here and now and
be done with it.'

ZAK. And what did she say?

HUMPY. She said 'Good riddance to bad rubbish', and she
walked away. 'Ha ha', says I to her, 'tickle me under the
arm and call me Geronimo.' Any sign of them?

ZAK. They're out around the Black Man.

HUMPY. Broaders sayin' hello to his granny again is he?

ZAK. Yeah.

VERONICA. He was dyin' alive about her wasn't he?

HUMPY. That's for sure. That was the only time I ever saw him
cryin' yeh know – at her funeral. Do yeh remember Zak?
The big red eyes on him. (*He chuckles.*) Here lies the body
of Marian Brennan who gave herself to the sea on the ninth
of November. Gone but not forgotten . . . She's alright there
though Missus, buried nearly next door to me Da there she is.

VERONICA. They keep the grave lovely anyway.

HUMPY. Broaders looks after that himself yeh know Missus –
fair play to him. I'm goin' to tell yeh one thing but it's a
pity Bridie wouldn't do the same with this one here. The
state of it! She comes up here every Sunday yeh know and
stands over this auld grave for hours on end, mutterin' to
herself. It'd match her better to clean it up a bit wouldn't it.
Put a bit of paint on it or somethin'. Look at the state of it!
Yeh can't read the writin' on the little cross nor nothin' . . .
Little Jimmy O'Keefe the baker was on his way to work the
mornin' Broaders' granny drown herself yeh know. He said
he saw her goin' down the bank – all dressed up like a dog's
dinner – and then she walked out into the water the same as
if she was goin' down the town. The man nearly died with
the fright boy! But sure auld Mosey is still not right yeh
know . . . Queer though ain't it?

VERONICA. Mmm . . .

HUMPY (*brushing back the briars and weeds from the little headstone*). St Martin's Eve 1986. Bridie's little bambino, hah! (*He chuckles.*)

Slight pause.

VERONICA (*going*). I'll see yeh lads.

ZAK. Yeah, right, Veronica.

HUMPY. All the best Missus. (*She goes.*) . . . Someone was tellin' me that she was seen down at the bar of the Railway Hotel last night drinkin' with your man Collins the teacher.

ZAK. No chance!

HUMPY (*sings*). Oh I am the village bicycle,
And they come from miles around . . . (*Taking out the diary.*) Hey Broaders, when is a secret not a secret? . . . When everybody knows about it! (*He laughs.*) . . . Wait 'til yeh hear this. 'Saw her today for the very first time – a magnificent looking woman with a mane of coal black hair and a pair of fiery eyes. She came to sell me a bucket of the loveliest lookin' oysters I've ever seen . . . '

Lights down.

Lights rise. EAGLE *and* ISAAC *are out in the boat, travelling beneath a starry sky, the light of the town behind them in the distance.*

ISAAC. Sure there's no such thing as wild boars in this country any more Da, is there?

EAGLE. No.

ISAAC. I knew that. Humpy O'Brien was tryin' to tell me that he came out here one day last week and found all this wild boar shit all over the place.

EAGLE. Don't mind him. Sure St Patrick drove the wild boars out of here years ago, son.

ISAAC. St Patrick drove the snakes out of Ireland, Da, not the wild boars.

EAGLE. Who told yeh that?

ISAAC. The teacher.

EAGLE. Yeah, well he drove the wild boars out as well. And, he told them all that they could take their shite with them, when they were goin'.

ISAAC *ponders.*

ISAAC. Well, if there's no wild boars here now any more, where did all the manure come from out on the island?

EAGLE. It was probably that auld pig that escaped from the bacon factory a few weeks ago there.

ISAAC. What did it do, Da, swim out there or somethin'?

EAGLE. Yeah, it swam out there.

ISAAC. And is it still out there, would yeh say?

EAGLE. No. To tell yeh the truth Isaac, he got so browned off out there that he swam back and gave himself up.

ISAAC. Our teacher was tellin' us that a pig can't swim very far without cuttin' his own throat, yeh know. He swims like this, Da. Kind of like a dog's paddle.

EAGLE. Isaac, will you sit down in the boat before yeh have the pair of us in the water.

ISAAC. Its nails are so sharp that he ends up cuttin' his own throat. (*He runs his nails across* EAGLE's *throat.*) Ahhh . . .

EAGLE. Jaysus, that teacher of yours is a mine of information alright, ain't he?

ISAAC. Yeah, he knows everything, boy. Hey, Da, did the pig that escaped from the bacon pig factory end up cuttin' his own throat, would yeh say?

EAGLE. No, he got back alright.

ISAAC. How come? I mean to say, that's a fair auld distance for a pig to swim without cuttin' its own throat, aint't it?

EAGLE. Yeah, well yeh see, Isaac, this lad wasn't doin' the dog's paddle like yeh know. This fella was able to do the breast stroke.

Pause.

ISAAC. Look at all the stars, Da. Kind of electric stars. Not in the sky Da, in the water. What are they, anyway?

EAGLE. Phosphorus.

ISAAC. Phosphorus! I must tell them in school about that on Monday. I *bet* the teacher don't know about that.

EAGLE. I'm feckin' sure he don't know about it.

ISAAC. The size of that big eel boy! That fella'd nearly turn the boat over, wouldn't he! Hah? What would ya do if he turned the boat over, Da?

EAGLE. I don't know.

ISAAC. Can you swim, Da!

EAGLE. Of course I can swim.

ISAAC. Can yeh? What's your favourite stroke?

EAGLE. The Japanese flip-flop. Nothin' moves, only your tonsils.

ISAAC. Yeah. 'Help, help . . . ' A full moon, hah? Deadly lookin', ain't it?

EAGLE. Yeah, yeh'd get up in the middle of the night to look at it, sure.

ISAAC (*chuckles*). That's a good one, Da. You'd get up in the middle of the night to look at it. You'd hardly see it in the middle of the day, would yeh? You should have been a comedian boy!

Pause.

EAGLE. There she is, Isaac. Useless Island. There seems to be a bit of an auld fog comin' down around her, too.

ISAAC. Yeah, it's queer spooky lookin', ain't it?

EAGLE. Not at all.

ISAAC. I don't think me Ma is exactly over the moon about all of this, Da, is she?

EAGLE. No. Not exactly. Ah, she's a bit nervous about it. Yeh see, Isaac, what she don't understand is that you and mc arc in our element out here, like yeh know. What she don't seem to realise is that this is our what-do-you-call-it . . . What's the word . . . Domain! But sure, I suppose she's listenin' to the rest of them blackguardin' me all the time. I'm not coddin' yeh, for the past twelve months here, you'd swear I was committin' some sort of a crime here just comin' out to work. I mean to say, I'm only doin' what I always done. Yeh know? I come out here and I cast me nets and I sit and wait. What's wrong with that? Yeh know? No way am I in the wrong. I don't care what anyone says. Yeh know sometimes when I'm out here on me own in the middle of the night I'll stand up in the boat like this – sometimes in the middle of the day, even – I'll stand up and I let a bit of an auld shout out of me. (*He shrieks.*) I'm not coddin' yeh. If anyone was watchin' me, they'd have me feckin' certified, so they would. But do yeh know why I do that? I do it to let this place know that I'm still here, that I'm still around. That's very important, yeh know! That way the man learns to respect the place and the place'll respect the man. Me Da taught me that . . . take a look back at the town.

ISAAC. Oh, yeah . . . All the lights! I wonder where our house is? I think I can see my pigeon loft, Da.

EAGLE *smiles at him tenderly.*

EAGLE. As long as you do your best, Isaac, that's all that matters, yeh know. You must always do your best. And make the most of what yeh got . . . What's that? A seagull flyin' low, be Jaysus?

ISAAC. What does that mean?

EAGLE. Search me.

He chuckles and sits down again.

Pause.

ISAAC. Do yeh know somethin', Da, I don't think I ever saw you swimmin' . . . Da?

EAGLE. What?

ISAAC. I say I never saw you swimmin'.

EAGLE. Why should I swim when I've got a boat?

Pause. Lights down.

ACT TWO

Useless Island . EAGLE is sitting beside a blazing log-fire just in front of the hut. He is drinking a bottle of stout and singing joyfully. ISAAC *is unpacking one of the cardboard boxes.*

EAGLE (*sings*).
 My heart is in Rosa Rio
 Under the Argentine Skies.
 There lives a beautiful lady
 With dark and sparkling eyes

 EAGLE *turns to look at his son.*

 What do yeh think of the bed I built for yeh?

ISAAC (*going into the hut*). Grand.

EAGLE. Yeah? There's an auld nail above it there in case you be wantin' to hang anythin' up. Do yeh see it?

ISAAC. Yeah. I just hit me head off of it.

 EAGLE *sniggers.* ISAAC *comes back out.*

ISAAC. Hey Da, will you be able to leave me that big flashlight before yeh go?

EAGLE. Yeah if yeh like. But sure yeh won't need it anyway Isaac. Before I'm done this fire'll light up the whole island for yeh boy.

ISAAC. Oh yeah, me Ma told me to tell yeh that the firelighters are in that auld brown bag there.

EAGLE. Firelighters! Do I look like a fella who needs firelighters to light a fire? Now first things, go get a cup and pull over.

ISAAC. What? Now?

EAGLE. Yeah. Now.

ISAAC *gets a mug from one of the boxes and* EAGLE *pours some stout into it. He then proceeds to put a few spoonfuls of sugar into it.*

EAGLE. Firelighters! Here, get that into yeh. It'll put a few hairs on your chest.

ISAAC. I love the way it all bubbles up when yeh put the sugar into it, do you? Is this part of the tradition too Da, yeah?

EAGLE. Sort of.

ISAAC. What do yeh mean, sort of?

EAGLE. Well my Da did somethin' like this too, the night he brought me out here. Mind you it wasn't exactly like this. He drank about seven large bottles of stout before he went home, Jaysus he was an awful man.

ISAAC. And did he give you a drop in the end of a mug too?

EAGLE. He gave me a whole small bottle to meself so he did. I was half-fluthered drunk before he was gone at all.

ISAAC. What did yeh do after he was gone? Were yeh afraid?

EAGLE. What? No way, José. No chance boy! I'll tell yeh now Isaac exactly what I done. I staggered into me hut and I snored like an auld fella all night long.

ISAAC. This'll make me snore Da, won't it?

EAGLE. It'll make yeh fart anyway. Whatever about snorin'.

ISAAC (*singing*). My fart is in Rosa Rio
Under the Argentine skies,

EAGLE (*singing*). There lives a beautiful lady
And I bless her the day that I die.
Aye, aye, aye, aye, aye, aye . . .
My heart is in Rosa Rio.

Pause.

ISAAC. Do yeh know somethin' Da, I heard that auld Mosey Brennan saw a mermaid out here one time! Just over there somewhere she was, baskin' in the sun, combin' her hair or somethin'.

EAGLE. Yeah?

ISAAC. What would yeh do though Da if yeh came out one mornin' and found a mermaid tangled up in your net?

EAGLE. What would I do? I'll tell yeh now son I'd throw her back into the sea the same as if she was an auld eel.

ISAAC. Are yeh mad or what, Da. The mermaid I'm talkin' about now is (*He moulds her shape.*) Yeh know. She's really beautiful.

EAGLE. I don't care what she looks like. Half a woman'd be no use to a man like me yeh know . . . Yeh might throw another log on that auld fire there will yeh?

ISAAC. Right.

EAGLE (*sings*) . My heart is in Rosa Rio,
Under the Argentine skies . . .

ISAAC. Why couldn't we come out here in the middle of the summer or somethin'. Da. I mean to say it's freezin' cauld out here now.

EAGLE. But sure any Jack the Shillin' could come out here in the middle of summer. That's what always amused me about Dribbler and Matty O'Brien and all. They came out here in the middle of summer. I mean to say where's the point in that. You came out here the same night I did – the tenth of November, St. Martin's Eve. Dribbler came out in August or somethin', August be Jaysus!

ISAAC. There's somethin' kind of special about St. Martin's Eve, Da ain't there?

EAGLE. Yeah. No self respectin' Wexford fisherman would ever cast a line on St. Martin's Eve.

ISAAC. Why not?

EAGLE. I don't know. They're superstitious about it. It's supposed to be unlucky or somethin'. Sure there's a song written about that and everythin'. 'The Fishermen of Wexford', it's called.

He sings.

There is an old tradition sacred held in Wexford town
That says upon St. Martin's Eve no net shall be let down.
No fishermen of Wexford shall upon that Holy Day
Set sail or cast a line within the scope of Wexford Bay.

The tongue that framed the order or the time no one can tell
And no one ever knew it but the people kept it well
And never in man's memory was fisher known to leave
The little town of Wexford on the good St. Martin's Eve.

That song was written about a disaster that happened here
one time. A few fleets decided to disregard that auld
tradition and go out fishin' on Martin's Eve. Seventy men
were lost that day from this little town alone boy. That's the
last line of the song in fact. 'Seventy Fishers' Corpses Strew
the Shores of Wexford Bay.'

ISAAC. Did you ever go out fishin' on St. Martin's Eve, Da?

EAGLE. I did. Once and once only. I had a bit of a fire in me
belly about somethin' and I refused to listen to anyone. I
lived to regret it though I can tell you.

ISAAC. Why? What happened?

EAGLE. What? Ah I had a bit of bad luck . . .

Slight pause.

ISAAC. Yeh might tell us about the Dempsey Twins again, Da,
will yeh?

EAGLE. The Dempsey Twins?

ISAAC. Yeah, tell us about them again. I loves hearin' about
them boy!

EAGLE. Do yeh? . . . The Dempsey Twins used to live around
the corner from your granny there, that little house that
what-do-you-call-its are livin' in now.

ISAAC. The Byrne's.

EAGLE. Yeah. They were more or less the same age as meself
and they were absolutely the spittin' image of one another.
The only way I was able to tell them apart was that one of
them had a slight cast in his eye. And they were inseparable

I'm not coddin' yeh. Always together the pair of them. In all the time I knew them I don't think I ever saw one without the other.

ISAAC. And supposin' one of them was sick would the two of them stay home from school?

EAGLE. Oh yeah. They wouldn't stir without one another sure. They walked the same, talked the same, dressed the same and everythin'.

ISAAC. Just a minute! Are you tryin' to tell me that if one of them was sick the two of them'd stay home from school?

EAGLE. Are you goin' to let me tell this story or not?

ISAAC. Yeah alright, go ahead.

EAGLE. The two boys were so inseparable that when it came to their turn to go out to the island their Da started kind of wonderin' if maybe it might be alright for them to go out together, seein' how they were never apart before, seein' how they were practically the same fella anyway. But unfortunately their Da was a bit of a pasty-faced sort of a fella – yeh know he was good around the house and all – with the result that nobody really liked him and everybody started sayin' that if the young lads were goin' to go out to the island then it was only right they should go out there alone the same as all the other young lads around here had done. So that's what they done in the end. I'll never forget that night though. The auld shingly beach thronged with people – most of us half hopin' to see the two boys goin' berserk or somethin'. But they didn't. They never even flinched boy. The little lad with the cast in his eye just stood beside his mother while the other lad climbed into the boat alongside his Da. One of the other men had to row out to the island because your man was useless with boats.

To make a long story short anyway in the middle of the night the little lad with the cast in his eye got up out of bed and went down to the water's edge. He could hear his brother cryin' and callin' out his name from the other side. He got so distressed that he kicked off his shoes and tried to swim across to the island just to be near him. But he ran into trouble about half way across and the little lad on the island jumped in and tried to swim to his rescue. Three days later the two dead bodies were fished out of the water.

Auld Mosey Brennan found them tangled up in one of his nets – clingin' together like an auld oyster around a pearl. And I'm goin' to tell yeh one thing but the day they were buried there wasn't a man or woman up around here that didn't hang their heads in shame. Auld Bridgey Malloy said that the poor crators died just because their Da had a pasty face.

Silence.

ISAAC. Well there's twin brothers in my class and they can't stand one another.

EAGLE. Listen you don't forget what your Mammy was sayin' to yeh about stayin' away from that fire do yeh hear me?

ISAAC. Yeah.

EAGLE. And yeh needn't bother your arse goin' down near that water's edge either. There's fifty feet of water there if not more. So stay away from it altogether. Do yeh hear me talkin' to yeh?

ISAAC. Yeah . . . What time will you be comin' back to collect me at?

EAGLE. The first thing in the mornin' I'll be back out for yeh. It's a pity yeh didn't think of bringin' your big ghetto blaster out with yeh ain't it?

ISAAC. Yeah, I forgot all about that.

EAGLE. But sure yeh can always read a couple of your comics can't yeh?

ISAAC. Yeah. As soon as I finish me porter now I'll read a couple of me comics.

EAGLE. Have yeh got everythin' out of me boat now yeah?

ISAAC. Yeah! I think so. Why, are yeh goin' now?

EAGLE. Yeah, I've to go now. Will you be alright?

ISAAC. Yeah.

EAGLE. Are yeh sure?

ISAAC. Yeah.

EAGLE. That's good because I've to go and drink a toast to yeh now on the mainland yeh see.

EAGLE looks into his son's sad eyes.

I was the last boy to come out here yeh know! (*Silence.*) I'll see yeh in the mornin', then Isaac, eh?

ISAAC. Yeah. Goodbye, Da.

EAGLE. Goodbye, son.

EAGLE leaves. Pause. Lights down.

*

Lights rise on the kitchen. A party is in full swing as DRIBBLER *sings and dances etc.*

DRIBBLER.
They came up from the country,
They came up from the farms.
They came up in their thousands
When they heard the call to arms.

I wanted to be a soldier boy,
To see what I could gain.
But when I put on the uniform,
It was then that I became

One of the old reserves,
One of the old reserves!
Up to the Curragh I was sent,
That's the place they pay no rent.

And when the sergeant saw me,
He said I did deserve
Three pints of beer Three times a day
For being one of the old reserves!

CHORUS.
>One of the old reserves,
>One of the old reserves
>One of the old, One of the old,
>One of the old reserves!

DRIBBLER.
>My first night in the cook house,
>My pal he said to me
>There's something wrong with the cook
>Because he's giving us eggs for tea.

>Now why he should make this rude remark
>I really couldn't tell.
>But when I opened up the egg,
>It was then that I got the smell!
>It was one of the old reserves
>One of the old reserves!

>To eat this egg I did my best,
>It nearly paralysed my chest.
>For a cook to cook an egg like that
>A shooting he deserved.
>But we let him go because we know
>He was one of the old reserves!

CHORUS.
>One of the old reserves, One of the old reserves,
>One of the old, One of the old,
>One of the old reserves!
>One of the old reserves, One of the old reserves
>One of the old, one of the old
>one
>of the
>old reserves.

Applause, laughter and general hubbub ensues.

MOSEY. Well done Dribbler.

ZAK. Oon, Dribbler me boy!

EAGLE. Fair play to yeh Drib . . .

DRIBBLER. Right lads, a bit of order there now. A bit of hush. Listen to me will yez. Order! I'm wantin' to propose a toast to Eagle and Isaac, lads.

MOSEY. Hear hear Dribbler!

DRIBBLER. Because what Eagle done tonight – bringin' Isaac out to the island and that – well I know it warmed the cockles of my heart anyway whatever about any of the rest of yeh and I'm sure Mosey Brennan there'll agree with me when I say that it's a pity the auld tradition ever died out in the first place.

MOSEY. That's for sure.

DRIBBLER. What it is lads is a gift. A gift from a father to a son. And on the eve of St. Martin's too hah!

BROADERS. St. Martin's eve, Dribbler, St. Martin's Eve boy!

DRIBBLER. Yeah that as well . . . no but seriously though lads. This is the kind of thing that can't be bought or sold yeh know. Yeh can't bottle it . . . Yeh can't wrap it up and put it on a shelf somewhere because it's not for sale. I mean to say I have fond memories meself of the night I spent out on the island. I brought me ferret out with me to keep me company and the little whore ran off huntin' in the bushes the minute I got there and I never saw him no more. A great big bull seal came up on to the island in the middle of the night then and started roarin' and bawlin' in the early hours – frightened the friggin' life out of me so he did. (*Laughter.*) But that was all a long time ago now though lads and things have changed. There was a time when you could look out that window there and you'd see thirty or forty little boats out there – sailin' across the bay after the herring or up the river after the salmon and the fresh water trout, or beyond the bar after the mullet and the mackerel. And in the evenin' they'd all pull into the shelter and you'd hear all the boys laughin' and jokin' and cursing and all. Marian Brennan'd come down with a bowl of soup for Mosey and Bridgey Malloy'd be callin' down to poor auld John-joe and you'd look up at the sky and yeh'd smell it and yeh'd taste it – the sea, and the wind and the rain – and back then there was no reason to believe that it was ever goin' to end but it did. Eagle there is the last of them now and here are we all workin' in the auld factory, fishin' for things we would have slung back once upon a time. We're all only – what's the word Eagle? Shadows of our former selves. That was nice Mosey wasn't it? But of course that's all neither here nor there now. Come on, raise your glasses. To Eagle and Isaac!

ALL. To Eagle and Isaac.

DRIBBLER. And to Veronica of course for puttin' up with the pair of them.

MOSEY. Well said, Dribbler.

They drink. VERONICA *is going round with a tray of food.*

DRIBBLER (*To* BROADERS) . He's one of the best boy. I don't care what anyone says . . .

BROADERS. Yeah but what's it all in aid of though Dribbler, that's what I'd like to know. What's it all in aid of?

DRIBBLER. Ah in aid of me arse! Put it there, Eagle. You're one in a million boy!

EAGLE (*wryly*). I am, ain't I?

DRIBBLER. Yeah. Yeh are though. I'm goin' to tell yeh one thing now Eagle for nothin' boy . . .

VERONICA. Don't strain yourself of anythin' there now Eagle.

EAGLE. What?

DRIBBLER. Hey Veronica, come here for a minute. (*He draws her towards him.*) Veronica'll vouch for me. She knows I don't bullshit.

VERONICA (*breaking*). Yeh don't? That's news to me then.

DRIBBLER. Hah? Lord Jaysus ain't that awful Eagle. Stymied at every fence boy. Hah? I don't know! No but seriously though Eagle. Straight up. You know me. If I say somethin' I mean it. If I don't mean it I won't say it, do yeh know what I mean?

EAGLE (*eating*). Yeah.

BROADERS. Hey Eagle I believe you're joinin' the firm on Monday mornin', is that right? Bright and early hah? You'll find out what hard work is all about then boy . . .

HUMPY. Yeah and yeh needn't think that this little escapade here tonight'll cut any ice either. Last in, first out boy.

DRIBBLER. Yeh may get used to all this Eagle because . . .

BROADERS. And here while we're on the subject, what's all this I hear about your missus being seen drinkin' with your man Collins the teacher last night down in the bar of the Railway Hotel? I hope you're not goin' to let the side down now or anythin' boy.

HUMPY. Yeah while you were out catchin' sardines Eagle she was out gettin' herself Edgamacated! (*He laughs.*) I hope yeh don't think that I was being impudent or anythin' there a minute ago Eagle, just markin' your card for yeh like yeh know. Last into the job, first out. Do yeh know what I mean Eagle?

EAGLE. Mmm . . . Jaysus people's atin' habits are terrible strange though lads ain't they?

HUMPY. Hah? How do yeh mean?

EAGLE. Well I mean yeh know how it is like. Some people go to restaurants and ate . . . Some people go to pubs. Other people love to be surrounded by people when they're atin'. Yeh know they go to dinner dances and what-do-you-call-its?

HUMPY. Reunions?

EAGLE. Yeah. They go to auld reunions and all. Now take me for example. When Eagle is atin' he just likes to be left alone. Do yeh know what I mean?

HUMPY. What?

BROADERS *chuckles and turns away.* HUMPY *stands there staring into* EAGLE's *eyes. Soon he gets the message and turns away sheepishly.*

*

Lights rise on the yard where ZAK *is sitting beneath a sliver of night blue sky.* VERONICA *comes out to collect a few empty plates and glasses etc.*

VERONICA. Are yeh not eatin' Zak?

ZAK. No. I'm not all that hungry to tell yeh the truth.

VERONICA. What's wrong with yeh? Sonia?

ZAK. It's a wonder she's here at all. Lately when I come in one door she goes out the other. I mean to say I can't even get a chance to what-do-you-call-it like yeh know . . . Ah I don't know. I asked Bridie to try and put in a word for me but . . . She thinks I should just let her go. What do you think?

VERONICA. I don't know Zak. Sonia's a bit of a Thumbelina Nolan I think.

ZAK. How do yeh mean?

VERONICA. She knows her way around.

ZAK. Does that mean that yeh think I have a chance with her?

VERONICA. Not really. (*She moves away.*)

Lights dim on the yard. Lights upon the kitchen. VERONICA *comes in from the yard with a handful of glasses and plates etc.*

BRIDIE. Are yeh alright Mosey?

MOSEY. Yeah. But sure it's grand to have a bit of grub handed to yeh ain't it?

BRIDIE. Mmn . . . Do yeh want a hand or anythin' Veronica?

VERONICA (*coldly*). No thanks.

BRIDIE *watches her going out into the yard again.*

BRIDIE. I dare say your auld house feels fairly quiet over there this weather Mosey is it?

MOSEY. Oh stop. It's like a grave sure. Not that meself and the missus ever did a whole lot of talkin' when she was alive anyway. A few auld grunts and growls now and again but nevertheless . . . To tell yeh the truth Bridie, the only noise you're likely to hear over there now is the sound of me askin' meself why she ever went and did what she done.

BRIDIE. But sure I suppose the poor crator was distracted Mosey.

MOSEY. Yeah. She must have been alright. Ah I don't think her heart was ever in that auld marriage from the start though yeh know. Her heart was elsewhere I think. I wouldn't mind but I knew that even in the early days only I was too bloody contrary to let her go. Mind you she was a beautiful sight to behold that time watchin' her risin' up before yeh in the mornin' or seein' her movin' about the house. I was kind of like a man with a beautiful flower that everyone else wanted, knowin' full well in me heart and soul that it was only a matter of time.

I used to pray that she'd wilt or wither a little bit just so I'd be allowed to hold on to her a little longer. But she never did. Not to my eyes anyway. And now I keep badgerin' poor little Jimmy O'Keefe the baker to try to tell me everything that he saw that mornin'. I'm sure the man dreads to see me comin' now. But I need to know why she gave herself up to the sea like that. I mean to say she always hated the sea. She hated it as much as I loved it yeh know. It's queer, ain't it? And here I am now another year and a day later and I'm still none the wiser and everything I thought I'd never be, I am.

BRIDIE. I wouldn't say you're none the wiser now, Mosey. Yeh found out what love is didn't yeh? What else is there to know?

MOSEY. Love? No, I don't think so somehow or other.

Lights dim on the kitchen. Lights up on the yard where EAGLE *and* VERONICA *are conversing.*

EAGLE. How many people were at the meetin'?

VERONICA. I don't know. Eight or nine.

EAGLE. And everyone went into the bar afterwards, did they?

VERONICA. No not everyone. Some of them went straight home and some of them went into the coffee shop.

EAGLE. How many went into the bar?

VERONICA. I don't know. I wasn't keepin' track of them.

EAGLE. How many? It was just you and him went into the bar wasn't it?

VERONICA. Yeah as far as I know . . .

EAGLE. What did yeh have?

VERONICA. I had a glass of lager.

EAGLE. How many drinks did yeh have?

VERONICA. Two or three.

EAGLE. Yeah and then what?

VERONICA. How do yeh mean?

EAGLE. Then what did yeh do?

VERONICA. We talked.

EAGLE. What did yeh talk about?

VERONICA. Look Eagle I really don't want to . . .

EAGLE. What did yeh talk about I said.

VERONICA. We talked about things. Different things. Things you wouldn't understand.

EAGLE. Oh things I wouldn't understand hah! All above my head! I had this tossed in my face here tonight yeh know in front of everyone. I mean to say this is exactly the kind of ammunition that they need to cut me off at the knees and here are you handin' it to them on a plate.

VERONICA. If you're not big enough to climb over those crowd of ejits Eagle, then I think you'll better stay out of the water by yourself where you belong.

EAGLE. What's that supposed to mean?

VERONICA. And you're talkin' about makin' a man out of Isaac. Jesus!

EAGLE. No, I'm talkin' about goin' round after school tomorrow and seein' this fella face to face, that's what I'm talkin' about.

VERONICA. You don't start anythin' here now.

EAGLE. That's what I'm talkin' about.

VERONICA. Eagle you go next or near that man and you'll be kissin' me goodbye boy.

EAGLE. Kissin' yeh goodbye. That'd make a change alright. Kissin' yeh goodbye or kissin' yeh hello either for that matter.

VERONICA. What's that supposed to mean? Eagle I'm a woman. And there's things I need to hear before I . . .

EAGLE. Things you need to hear! Well there's things I don't need to hear! . . . What do yeh think of that, Dribbler? There's things she needs to hear!

DRIBBLER. What's that?

VERONICA *throws* EAGLE *a dirty look.* EAGLE *grabs his coal and leaves in a huff.*

EAGLE. I'm goin' to take a bit of a walk Dribbler, I'll see yeh after.

DRIBBLER. Yeah right Eagle.

VERONICA *watches* EAGLE *go. Inside* BRIDIE *is singing 'I Let My Hair Down'.*

VERONICA. What am I goin' to do with that fella Dribbler eh?

DRIBBLER. I don't know. I've no sympathy for yeh, yeh couldn't wait to get him. I wouldn't mind but I was the one who saw yeh first.

VERONICA. Yeah? (*He nods.*) . . . So how come I ended up with him?

DRIBBLER.
  Why does the sun go down!
  I Let My Hair Down
  I slipped my shoes off
  Danced like an angel

  Lights down.

                          *

Lights rise on the island. ISAAC *is sitting over the fire reading
a comic. On a nearby hilltop* SONIA *and* BRIAN *are
snuggling into one another, looking down on the boy from afar.*

SONIA. Ah, look at the little face on him. He looks lost don't
  he?

BRIAN. Yeah. Cosy but lost. Are yeh wantin' to go down to
  him?

SONIA. No, we can't go down to him. Nobody's supposed to
  go near him tonight.

BRIAN. Well what did we come out here for then?

SONIA. Just to make sure that he's alright.

BRIAN. Really?

SONIA. Mm . . .

BRIAN. That fire looks nice.

SONIA. Sssh . . .

BRIAN. My hands are cold.

SONIA. Are they?

  She looks into his eyes and smiles. They kiss.

BRIAN. Now I'm beginnin' to see what me grandda saw in
  this place.

SONIA. What, the women yeh mean?

BRIAN. No, the harbour!

She plucks him playfully. He restrains her and they kiss.

I bet she looked just like you yeh know. Dark and beautiful. And a bit of a mystery! And when she walked down the street the whole whatdoyoucallit changed.

Awkward pause.

BRIAN. I don't think my grandda ever got over her yeh know, not according to that auld diary anyway. And he never really trusted anyone again after that either. He was so full of ire that he couldn't even bring himself to acknowledge his own grandchildren. He drove his whole family away sure. The only time I've ever seen a pair of eyes so angry was the other day when I was givin' Broaders a bollockin' for being late. Smoulderin' they were nearly! . . . I found these pictures of Menapia Mansion in an auld cardboard box yeh know. Little sort of postcards that were printed of it. It looked like a lovely place alright – the house, the gardens, even the factory had a certain flair to it.

He shakes his head and sighs.

SONIA. But sure maybe you'll put it all back together again hah?

BRIAN. Mm, that'd be somethin' alright wouldn't it? Put it all back together again and then when no one was lookin' just slip quietly away.

SONIA. I love it when you're serious. The little wrinkles around your eyes and all. And in the office when yeh put on your glasses. Sometimes I see yeh through the window. Yeh always look so intelligent or somethin'.

BRIAN. I am intelligent.

SONIA. Yeah but yeh don't always look it.

BRIAN. Thanks very much.

They cuddle into each other.

SONIA. Bridie says that I should try and hang on to you yeh know – that you'd make a good catch.

BRIAN. Is that what you're lookin' for – a good catch?

SONIA. Well I'm hardly lookin' for a bad one now am I?

BRIAN *laughs and lays his head in her lap.*

BRIAN. Jaysus, what have I let myself in for here eh?

SONIA. Yeah. You'd want to be careful Brian. The place is probably mined or somethin' yeh know.

They kiss. Lights down.

*

Lights rise. The graveyard. BROADERS, ZAK *and* HUMPY *enter, drinking from flagons of cider.*

HUMPY. Do yeh know what gets on my nerves Broaders? Bridie singin' that auld song all the time. The same auld song all the time she sings boy don't she? That gets on my nerves boy! And Dribbler is as bad. (*He sings scoffingly.*) 'One of the auld reserves, one of the auld reserves . . . ' It'd put years on yeh wouldn't it? Hah?

ZAK. Shut up Humpy will yeh, they're right behind us yeh know.

HUMPY. I'm worried about them now Zak!

BROADERS. Bullshit! That's what I hate.

HUMPY. What?

BROADERS. Bullshit! I look around me and all I see is bullshit. Grown men walkin' around with their tails between their legs be Jaysus I see Dribbler – bullshittin' and I see Eagle.

HUMPY. Bullshittin'.

BROADERS. I see Mosey.

HUMPY. Bullshittin'!

BROADERS. And Bridie!

HUMPY. Bullshittin'!

BROADERS. And I see me.

HUMPY. Bullshittin'.

BROADERS *throws him a dirty look.*

BROADERS. I see me inventin' a new language. A new way of lookin' at things.

HUMPY. How do yeh mean?

BROADERS. The mark of the crab!

HUMPY. Yes.

BROADERS (*holding his drink aloft*). To the mark of the crab!

HUMPY. Gullagullagoo.

BROADERS (*inhaling*). I need to do somethin', take somebody down a peg or two!

HUMPY. Yes!

HUMPY *grins with excitement.* DRIBBLER *and* BRIDIE *enter. She goes to the grave.*

DRIBBLER. That was a right auld stave though all the same lads wasn't it! Hah?

HUMPY. Bullshit Dribbler. A load of bullshit boy!

DRIBBLER. What? Well I enjoyed it anyway.

ZAK. And fuck the begrudgers Dribbler, ain't that right?

DRIBBLER. Exactly!

BROADERS. I'm goin' to tell yeh one thing Dribbler but the way you were goin' on tonight about Eagle, anyone'd think he was after walkin' on the water or somethin'.

DRIBBLER. I never said the man walked on the water at all.

BROADERS. I mean to say that's alright Dribbler but livin' in the past is all very well but I mean to say there's much more interestin' stories around than the ones you fellas keep tellin' us all the time yeh know. Stories of unborn bastards for instance and young women growin' old before their time . . . Night time stories Dribbler like yeh know. Night time stories boy!

HUMPY. Well, if it's night time stories you're wantin' Broaders, I'll give yeh a right one now. (*He takes out the diary.*) If I can find it . . . Hey Dribbler, he said he wanted to live inside of her!

DRIBBLER (*dark*). Yeah, who's that?

HUMPY. Taylor's grandda. Do yeh know what she died of Dribbler? Hornitus! Accordin' to this anyway.

DRIBBLER. What is that loola goin' on about eh?

BROADERS. I'm goin' to do somethin' . . . Come on, let's do something.

HUMPY. What? Where are yeh goin' Broaders.

BROADERS. Let's do somethin'.

HUMPY. Hah? Yes! Come on, Zak, we're goin' to do somethin'. Gullagullagoo . . . Hey Dribbler, a load of bullshit boy!

The three boys exit. Pause. DRIBBLER *turns to find* BRIDIE *standing over the little overgrown grave.*

DRIBBLER. What's up Bridie? Are yeh alright?

BRIDIE. Yeah.

DRIBBLER. What? . . . What's wrong?

BRIDIE. This is my baby's grave Dribbler.

DRIBBLER. Yeah I know.

BRIDIE. This is the first time you've ever come up here with me and this is my baby's grave. I know yeh think yeh love me and all. Yeh act as if yeh love me and yeh look as if yeh love me and yet this is the first time yeh ever visited the grave with me. Part of me is buried here too yeh know. It shapes nearly everythin' I do and say, everythin' I am really. And you've never been here before have yeh? My baby's grave! He must have been the quietest boy that ever was born. He came into the world and went back out of it again without makin' a sound. We buried him without a sound and I mourned him without a sound too – pacin' up and down me bedroom floor. Tiptoein' to work in the mornin's, everythin' kind of muffled. Days, weeks, months, years – everything muffled . . . And now it's the tenth of November

again – St. Martin's Eve – and this is my baby's grave. If he
had lived he would have been thirteen today – old enough to
go out to the island . . . And I'll tell yeh somethin' else for
nothin' Dribbler, it breaks my heart to think that his Daddy
has never even come here to say a few prayers for him or to
put a few flowers on his grave. Yes, this is my baby's grave
and not a day goes by that I don't think of him and mourn
for him. Not a day boy!

DRIBBLER. Sure I know that Bridie. Anyone who ever
listened to yeh singin'd know that . . . I'm goin' to tell yeh
one thing but I'm comin' up here tomorrow to clean up that
auld grave. And I'm goin' to paint that auld cross too, I
don't mind tellin' yeh. We should get a proper headstone for
here anyway. Sure who knows, maybe we'll all be lyin' in
there beside him one of these days hah?

BRIDIE *smiles through her tears. She blesses herself and
mouths a silent prayer. Pause. Lights down.*

*

Lights rise on the island. ISAAC *is sitting in front of his hut.
He rises, stretches himself and yawns. The wind rustles. He
picks up his flashlight and shines it into the bushes, singing to
hide his fear.*

ISAAC (*sings*). There is an old tradition
　　　Sacred held in Wexford Town
　　　That says upon St. Martin's Eve
　　　No net shall be let down.

*He gathers his things together and goes into the hut for the
night.*

No fishermen of Wexford
Shall upon that holy day
Set sail or cast a line.

Lights down.

*

Lights rise on the graveyard where EAGLE *is standing over the boy's grave. He has a catapult which he places on the grave. He blesses himself. A cold wind blows. Pause. He seems to hear a tune playing in the wild reeds – 'I Let My Hair Down'.*

Pause. Lights down.

*

Lights rise on the island. BROADERS *is kicking the fire alive.* ZAK *is sitting beside the hut, drinking.* HUMPY *is on the roof, howling like a wolf.* ISAAC *crawls out of the hut and shines his flashlight into* HUMPY*'s eyes.*

HUMPY. The face of him!

ISAAC. What are you doin' out here? No one's supposed to come out here tonight yeh know.

BROADERS. That's the thanks we get now lads.

ISAAC. What?

ZAK. It's alright Isaac, stop worryin' will yeh.

ISAAC. Stop worryin' he says!

BROADERS. So this is the famous hut then is it? We never saw one of these before yeh know. We were all deprived.

HUMPY. Yeah, we were all deprived. (*He pretends to weep.*) What kind of sandwiches have yeh got boy?

HUMPY *jumps down and takes* ISAAC*'s lunch box.*

ISAAC. Hey Humpy, give them back to me.

HUMPY (*eating a sandwich*). What?

ISAAC. Cut it out Humpy, they've to last me all night yeh know. I'll tell me Da on you in the mornin' boy.

HUMPY. Go ahead tell him, I don't care. I'm only feedin' the poor auld seagulls anyway. Here chuck. Here chuck, chuck, chuck . . .

BROADERS. So tell us how does it feel to be a man boy? Do yeh feel it all seepin' through yeh now yeah? Hah? Do yeh? Yeah? Hah?

He crowds ISAAC.

ISAAC. Go away from me Broaders will yeh.

BROADERS. Hah?

HUMPY. Are these all the comics yeh have?

ZAK. Bad news for yeh Isaac, it looks like I'm not goin' to be your uncle after all.

HUMPY. Yeah so give him back all the money he gave yeh . . .

BROADERS. Hey boy, I hope you don't think that this is going to make you a big shot around here now or anythin'. Just because you're the only one to come out here and all.

ZAK. But sure he is the only one. Ain't yeh, Isaac?

ISAAC. I don't know I suppose I am. But sure me Da was the last boy to come out here yeh know – before me I mean.

BROADERS *laughs.*

ISAAC. What's so funny Broaders, he's better than you anyway.

BROADERS. Oh yeah? In what way like?

ISAAC. Every way.

BROADERS. In what way is he better than me though?

ISAAC. Every way I said.

BROADERS. What?

ISAAC. He goes his own way and that.

BROADERS. He goes his own way?

ISAAC. Yeah.

BROADERS. What do yeh mean he goes his own way like?

ISAAC. He goes his own way that's all. He don't have to answer to no one nor nothin'.

BROADERS. Why who do I have to answer to?

ISAAC. Yeh have to answer to your boss – the fella that owns the factory or whatever yeh want to call him.

BROADERS. But sure your Da'll have to start answerin' to him next week.

ISAAC. How do yeh mean?

BROADERS. Your Da is turnin' into work in the factory on Monday mornin' boy. Bright and early!

ISAAC. Who told you that? He never said nothin' to me about that then.

BROADERS. Yeah well he wouldn't would he? That's what this is all in aid of sure. You've been bought and sold down the river boy so yeh have.

ISAAC. I don't believe you.

BROADERS. Suit yourself.

ISAAC *looks from* BROADERS *to* ZAK *to* HUMPY.

ISAAC. Go away, yeh liar Broaders!

BROADERS (*viciously grabbing* ISAAC *by the wrists*). Now you listen to me boy, Broaders may be a whole lot of things but one thing he never is is a liar and don't you ever forget that.

BROADERS *releases* ISAAC *and seeing the medallion he rips it from* ISAAC*'s neck. He turns away towards the fire.*

ZAK (*singing*).
There is an old tradition
Sacred held in Wexford Town
That says upon St. Martin's Eve
No net shall be let down.

ISAAC *feels his sore wrists.*

Yeh missed a right session in the pub tonight Isaac.

ISAAC. Yeah? Why was there a bit of a singsong there and all yeah?

ZAK. Yeah there was a right singsong there boy. We all drank a toast to you and all sure.

ISAAC. Who was there?

ZAK. Everyone. Mosey and Dribbler and all. A right session it was, boy.

ISAAC. Did Dribbler sing 'One of the Old Reserves?'

ZAK. Yeah.

ISAAC. And did he do all the actions to it and all?

ZAK. The whole works boy. And your Da sang 'The Fishermen of Wexford'.

ISAAC. Did he? That's a deadly song ain't it?

ZAK. Deadly!

HUMPY (*chuckling at the comic*). Look at the little skinny head on your man, Isaac.

ISAAC. Who? Show us. Oh yeah, I loves him. There's a lad in my class and he has a head just like that yeh know.

HUMPY. Your man has a neck like a corkscrew hasn't he?

ZAK. What are yeh doin' Broaders, countin' the stars or what?

BROADERS. What?

ZAK. Can yeh see what it's all in aid of out there yeah?

HUMPY (*pointing to the comic*) . What do that mean?

ISAAC. Von't. So yeh von't talk hah?

HUMPY. Von't.

ISAAC. He's a German Humpy. A Nazi! So yeh von't talk hah?

HUMPY (*bewildered*). Hah? How can the man talk and be gagged?

ISAAC. Exactly!

    ZAK *lilts the tune of 'The Fishermen of Wexford' as* BROADERS *examines the medallion.*

BROADERS. Me granny used to bring me out here every year for a day when I was a young fella yeh know. 'We're goin' out to the Island tomorrow,' she'd say out of the blue as if she had just got an invisible signal or somethin'. And I'd be sent off to the shop for the lemonade and biscuits while she made the sandwiches. Me grandda Mosey'd drop us off here on his way to work and meself and me granny'd go tiptoein' around this auld island like a couple of intruders . . . She used to stand on top of that little hill over there. She'd close her eyes and let the wind blow through her hair. She'd pick up a handful of sand and watch it tricklin' through her fingers. She'd hold a queer lookin' shell against her ear and listen to the sea. Later on I'd go prowlin' around the island and she'd sit over there somewhere readin' a book and every time I'd sneak up behind her I'd find her starin' into space, the book lyin' open in her lap, miles away! . . . And I'd crouch down behind an auld wall and call out to her, Marian Meek and Mild . . . It was out here one day that she made me promise her that when I was old enough I'd sprout a pair of wings and fly away. She showed me a paintin' of a white winged horse and I used to picture meself flyin' off on it – up over the town, up over the houses, away over, the island. And I'd hear her callin' out to me to never come back. 'You don't belong here,' she said 'Go away and never come back' . . . Never come back! Of course I didn't know then that she was goin' to go away without me. I always thought she'd be here to see me go.

Silence.

ZAK (*reciting*).
There is an old tradition sacred in Wexford Town
That says upon St. Martin's Eve no net shall be let down.
No fisherman of Wexford shall upon that holy Day
Set sail or cast a line within the scope of Wexford Bay.

He begins to beat out a rhythm on an old wooden box. After a while HUMPY *becomes infected and he too begins to beat an old tin can. There is something savage about the sound.*

The tongue that framed the order or the time no man can tell
And no one ever knew it but the people kept it well

For never in man's memory was fisher known to leave.
The little town of Wexford on the good St. Martin's Eve.

The rhythm climbs towards a savage crescendo.

Alas! Alas for Wexford! Once upon that holy Day
Came a wondrous shoal of herring to the waters of the bay
The fishers and their families stood out upon the beach
And all day watched with wistful eyes the wealth they
    might reach.
Such shoals were never seen before and keen regret went
    round.
Alas! Alas for Wexford! Hark! What is that grating sound?
The boat's keel on the shingle, Mothers! Wives ye well may
    grieve
The fishermen of Wexford mean to sail on Martin's Eve.

The drumming is at feverish pitch now. SONIA *enters with*
BRIAN *trailing slightly behind her.*

'Oh stay ye,' cried the women wild
'Stay!' cried the men white-haired
And dare ye not to do the thing your fathers never . . .

The song trails off at the sight of SONIA *and* BRIAN
approaching. HUMPY *does not see them and continues to*
drum.

BROADERS. Well what do yeh know Isaac, Aunty Sonia and
Uncle Whatishisname have come to pay a call.

ISAAC. What? Ah for God's sake, what is this a feckin'
reunion or somethin'?

HUMPY. Hey Isaac, I thought no one was supposed to come
out here tonight.

ISAAC. What are youse wantin'?

SONIA. Now Isaac don't get excited. Calm down. What are
you doin' out here Zak?

ZAK. What am I doin' out here! (*He shakes his head in*
disgust.)

BROADERS (*sticking his knife in the fire*). It's alright Sonia.
We only came out to make sure that the young fella was

alright like yeh know. Yeh see sometimes these courtin'
couples come out here to screw in the bushes and that, and
we just thought Isaac might get a bit of a fright when he'd
hear them gruntin' and groanin' like yeh know.

HUMPY *titters.*

BRIAN. What's goin' on?

BROADERS. And the dead arose and appeared to many.

BRIAN. What?

BROADERS. I was just sayin' here Mister New Boss that we
only came out to try and bring it home to Isaac that this
heap of shite that he's been sleepin' in tonight is no longer
what-do-you-call-it around here any more . . . What's the
word, Zak? Valid! That's it. It's out of date. Old hat! Yeah.
This is the baby now if you're wantin' to keep abreast of
things around here. The mark of the crab!

HUMPY. Yes!!

BROADERS. So we decided to come out and initiate Isaac
into the gang. Ain't that right Isaac?

ISAAC. No way Broaders! I'm not lettin' you next or near my
arm, boy.

BROADERS. What?

SONIA. I think we're goin' to have to take Isaac back into
town with us.

BRIAN. Alright.

ISAAC. Into town! I can't go back into town until the mornin'.

SONIA. Look Isaac, I'll explain it to your Daddy when we get
home.

ISAAC. Ah Sonia . . .

BROADERS. It's reddenin' up Isaac.

ISAAC. What?

BROADERS. It's reddenin'up.

ISAAC. Will you shut up Broaders and leave me alone.

BROADERS (*taking the red hot knife out of the fire*). Oh yes, I think so.

BRIAN. Cut it out Broaders will yeh, you're frightenin' the young fella.

BROADERS (*pulling the knife back into the fire again*). What?

BRIAN. Cut it out I said.

BROADERS (*rising*). You must think that you're still in the factory or somethin' do yeh? Givin' orders there!

BRIAN. Get your things together Isaac and come on.

ISAAC. Tch . . . (*He begins to gather up his belongings.*)

BROADERS (*shoving* BRIAN *around, trying to humiliate him*). Yes, givin' orders there if yeh don't mind. Givin' orders. Who do you think yeh are, eh boy? I mean to say you're not in the factory now or anythin' yeh know. Givin' orders.

BRIAN. Grow up, Broaders, will yeh.

BROADERS. A hard case with a soft suitcase there, givin' orders.

SONIA. Leave him alone, Broaders.

BROADERS. Mouth almighty, givin' orders.

HUMPY *titters.*

ISAAC. I'm goin' to tell me Da on you in the mornin' Broaders.

BRIAN. Come on Isaac, will yeh.

ISAAC. Yeah, just a minute.

SONIA. Hurry up Isaac.

BROADERS. You must think that yeh own the place up around here now or somethin' do yeh?

BRIAN. No I don't think I own the place at all.

BROADERS. What?

BRIAN *looks to see* BROADERS *staring into his eyes. Silence.* BROADERS *sniggers and begins to walk away, turning quickly to punch* BRIAN *in the stomach then hitting him with a rabbit punch on the back of the neck as he goes down.* HUMPY *immediately pounces on him, yelping as he proceeds to kick* BRIAN *viciously in the side and sitting on his back and forcing his face into the dirt and so on.* SONIA *runs between them but she is thrown to the ground.* ZAK *tries to separate them too.*

ZAK. That's enough Broaders. Take it easy will yeh.

SONIA. Broaders! Come up off him Humpy.

BROADERS. Yes, givin' orders there if yeh don't mind.

HUMPY. I'll tell yeh what we'll do Broaders we'll tie him up with his own tie. And then we'll give him the mark of the crab, seein' how he has a burnin' desire to be one of us. On the forehead, so everyone can see it.

HUMPY *ties* BRIAN*'s hands behind his back with the tie that he has ripped from around* BRIAN*'s neck.*

ISAAC (*calling out*). Da! Da! Help Da!

SONIA. You do Broaders and I swear . . .

BRIAN. Let me up Humpy. Come up off of me I said.

HUMPY. Do yeh hear him Broaders. Givin' orders again. You're in no position to give anybody any orders. (*He takes out the diary.*) First I'm goin' to read you a little night time story. Do you recognize this? (*He sniggers.*) Right. 'She uttered the immortal words to me again last night, "I love you too," I said, as the night came down around us . . . ' But unfortunately bad news for him on the very next page. 'She never showed up last night. Something is wrong I'm afraid .' That was July fourth. 'July the fifth. Still no sign of her. Where can she be. It's over I think. I've lost her. And I'm lost without her. ' Oh yes I'm afraid this little lady was neither meek nor mild . . . What do yeh make of that? Your grandda was sufferin' from a severe case of . . .

BROADERS *face darkens. He leaves the blade in the fire and comes across to snatch the diary from* HUMPY*'s hand. He reads it and with a furious roar throws it out to sea.*

HUMPY. Hey Broaders, what are yeh doin' boy.

BROADERS (*pulling back* BRIAN*'s head.*) You leave things where they fall in future Mister. Hold his head back there Humpy.

HUMPY. Yes!

SONIA. Zak, you'd better stop them. Do yeh hear me Zak.

ZAK. That's enough Broaders, the game's over.

BROADERS (*at the fire*). Hah?

ZAK. The game's over I said. Come up off of him Humpy.

ZAK *grabs* HUMPY *by the hair and throws him to the ground.*

ZAK. Come up off him I said.

BROADERS. Is there somethin' wrong with you Zak?

ZAK. No, there's nothin' wrong with me at all. You're the one who wants to take a good look in the mirror at himself boy, not me.

ZAK *bends to untie* BRIAN*'s hands.*

BROADERS. What are yeh doin' Zak?

ZAK. I'm lettin' him go. Isaac get your things and bring them down to the boat.

BROADERS. Leave him.

ZAK. What?

BROADERS. Leave him I said. I'm goin' to brand that bastard. Hold his head back Humpy.

HUMPY. What?

BROADERS. Hold his head.

ZAK (*rising*). Don't start now Broaders.

BROADERS. Why?

ZAK. Because the game's over that's why.

BROADERS. Turnin' against us now are we?

ZAK. Yeah, if helpin' the man up and down to the boat is turnin' against yeh then yeah I'm turnin' against yeh. Alright? Are yeh satisfied now?

BROADERS. I'm goin' to tell yeh one thing Zak but you're some turncoat alright boy.

ZAK (*bending to untie* BRIAN'*s hands*). Yeah, sure.

Suddenly BROADERS *in a fit of rage raises the knife and brings it down into* ZAK'*s shoulder.* ZAK *cries out in pain and falls to the ground.* ISAAC *runs to the hill top.* SONIA *follows him.*

ISAAC (*from the hilltop*). Da! Da! Help Da . . . Help!

BROADERS *hovers over* ZAK *who instinctively crawls away from his shuffling feet.*

BROADERS. That's it Zak, you crawl on your belly boy. Slither like an auld eel there, that's all you were ever any good for anyway. Well not Broaders. I'll crawl for no one nor nothin'. Never! And I'll answer to no one either. Because if you think now Zak that I'm goin' to stand around listenin' to some auld fella yearnin' for the past then you've another think comin' to yeh boy. The here and now is what matters to me mate. Now! Right now! Today! So while you're sittin' here waitin' for Judgement Day to come I'm goin' to be out there take, take takin' all the time. Because this is the bottom of the barrel we're all slidin' around in now Zak yeh know. The greedy bastards took it all and left us nothin'. Except this of course. (*The hut.*) I forgot all about this – our inheritance! Well do yeh want to know what I think about this Zak? Here's what I think about it.

He goes into the hut and proceeds to wreck it.

That's what I think, of that . . . Queer ignorant ain't I? A real savage boy! But yeh see the problem is Zak I don't believe in fairy tales any more like yeh know! (*He shrugs.*)

ISAAC (*from the hilltop*). Da! Da! Help Da! Help . . .

Pause. BROADERS *turns and gazes up to the heavens, his eyes brimming with tears.*

BROADERS. 'Go away and never come back,' she said . . . Never come back!

ISAAC. Help Da, Help! . . .

SONIA (*calls out*). Eagle!

BROADERS (*looking into* BRIAN's *frightened eyes*). What are you lookin' at? What's the matter, are yeh wantin' to make sure that you'll know me the next time we meet or somethin', is that it? Well here – just so you'll know me.

BROADERS *takes the hot knife and holds it to* BRIAN's *head. He looks deep into* BRIAN's *eyes and seems to see himself there. Then suddenly he takes the red hot blade and holds it to his own forehead. He roars out in pain and slowly sinks to his knees, burying his head in the dirt to stifle his cries.* SONIA *runs to free* BRIAN's *hands.* HUMPY *stands there stunned.* ISAAC *runs back to* SONIA's *arms.*

Slowly BROADERS *raises his head to reveal the mark of the crab burnt into his forehead. He rises from his knees, backs away in shame and dropping the knife turns to flee. Pause. Lights down.*

*

Lights rise on the kitchen. EAGLE *is sitting at the table.* MOSEY *is sitting by the door.* SONIA *enters.*

SONIA. How his he?

EAGLE. Alright. He's up in the bed there.

SONIA. Me heart . . . Any sign of Broaders yet?

EAGLE. No. Just as well. 'Cause I'd have kilt him if I'd a caught him last night Mosey.

MOSEY. What gets into that fella at all eh? I don't know where he gets it out of . . . Mind you.

EAGLE. Huh?

VERONICA *comes down the stairs.*

SONIA. How is he?

VERONICA. Alright. He's wantin' another cup of tea. How did Zak get on after?

SONIA. A couple of stitches.

VERONICA. Did they keep him in yeah?

SONIA. No, he signed himself out sure.

VERONICA *shrugs.*

VERONICA. What about Brian? (*She fills a hot water bottle.*)

SONIA. What about him?

VERONICA. Well what happened to him like?

SONIA. I don't know. I forgot all about him to tell you the truth.

VERONICA. He must think we're all mad up around here or somethin'.

SONIA. Yeah. He's probably after runnin' for the hills by now I'd say.

EAGLE (*rising*). Away with him! I'll bring that up to him Veronica.

VERONICA. Huh? Oh yeah right.

Pause.

Go ahead.

EAGLE. Is he not wantin' any toast with this or anything no?

VERONICA. No, he's not wantin' nothin' with it.

EAGLE. Fair enough . . . There is an old tradition Mosey huh?

MOSEY. What's that? Yeah . . . Sacred held in Wexford town!

EAGLE *exits. Lights down.*

*

Lights rise. DRIBBLER *is in the little graveyard . . . clipping the grass on the grave etc. The cross has been painted white. He finds the catapult and wonders about it.*

ISAAC. Here y'are Dribbler, me Mammy sent these up to yeh. (*A bunch of wild flowers.*)

DRIBBLER. Oh right, thanks Isaac. Put them there in that auld urn will yeh . . . An eventful night last night by all accounts?

ISAAC. Yeh, it surely was. Them fellas are all mad Dribbler! I wouldn't mind but nobody was supposed to come next or near me last night yeh know.

DRIBBLER. Yeah well I wouldn't worry too much about that if I was you Isaac. From what I was told I think yeh came through it all with flyin' colours boy. Yes flyin' colours!

He gives ISAAC *the catapult.*

ISAAC. Did yeh hear what Broaders did?

DRIBBLER. Yeah.

ISAAC. Broke up me little hut and everything he did. I'm goin' to tell yeh one thing Dribbler but he was queer lucky that me Da didn't catch him this mornin' because he'd've kilt him. Mosey thinks he's after headin' for London or somewhere. He burnt the mark of the crab into his forehead yeh know.

DRIBBLER. So I heard. He'd be a nice sight to behold now down around Camden Town or somewhere wouldn't he? Hah?

ISAAC. Me Da gave Humpy O'Brien the greatest kick in the arse he ever got boy. And the blood was pumpin' out of the other fella.

DRIBBLER. Who's that?

ISAAC. Zak. Sonia went off in the ambulance with him yeh know.

DRIBBLER. Aye?

ISAAC. That's lookin' alright now Dribbler ain't it? (*The grave.*)

DRIBBLER. Not bad.

ISAAC. Did yeh know me Da is turnin' in the factory on Monday?

DRIBBLER. Yeah, I know.

ISAAC. You'll all be workin' there then Dribbler.

DRIBBLER. Yeah . . . by the time you're old enough to manage the factory we'll have the place hoppin' for yeh so we will.

ISAAC. Me workin' there! You must be jokin' Dribbler. No way boy!

DRIBBLER. Why, what are yeh goin' to do instead?

ISAAC. I don't know. I'm not goin' to work there anyway, that's for sure. I'll probably go out fishin' Dribbler, like the Da used to do.

I'd say I'd make a good fisherman though Dribbler would you? Hah?

DRIBBLER. Yeah.

ISAAC. I will boy!

ISAAC *aims and fires the catapult. Lights down.*